LAKE GEORGE REFLECTIONS

LAKE GEORGE REFLECTIONS

ISLAND HISTORY AND LORE

Best wishes

Frank Leonbruno

BY FRANK LEONBRUNO

WITH GINGER HENRY

PURPLE MOUNTAIN PRESS • FLEISCHMANNS, NEW YORK

Published by
Purple Mountain Press, Ltd.
Main Street, P.O. Box E3
Fleischmanns, New York 12430-0378
(914) 254-4062
FAX (914) 254-4476

These chapters (with the exception of "The Saga of the Lake George Trout")
originally were published as articles in *The Chronicle*, Glens Falls, N.Y.
Maps © The National Survey, Inc., Chester, Vermont. Used by permission.

Library of Congress Cataloging-in-Publication Data
Leonbruno, Frank, 1918–
    Lake George reflections : island history and lore / Frank Leonbruno
with Ginger Henry. — 1st ed.
        p.   cm.
    ISBN 0-935796-97-5 (pbk.)
    1. George, Lake (N.Y. : Lake)—History.   2. Islands—New York (State)—Lake
George (Lake)—History.   3. Leonbruno, Frank, 1918– .   I. Henry, Ginger, 1949– .
II. Title.
F127.G3L6   1998
974.7'51—dc21   98-7370
                                                                             CIP

Page design and typesetting: Jerry Novesky

Manufactured in the United States of America

Frontis: Frank Leonbruno in his park ranger uniform, 1944.
Cover photo © Dean Color, Glens Falls, N.Y.

CONTENTS

Acknowledgments

Without the assistance of my many friends, this book never would have been possible. I owe a tremendous debt of gratitude to the individuals listed below who not only helped me in my work but also gave me the inspiration to record my memoirs of the lake that has been my love, my passion, and my livelihood for most of my life.

It was Dr. Robert Rosen who originally convinced me to put pen to paper.

Zandy Gabriels donated a great deal of time putting the first draft of the book into the computer and suggesting changes to the text.

Jane Gabriels, Zandy's mother, provided me with information and moral support.

Dick and Pat Swire, residents of Three Brother Islands, were also of great help, offering both editorial input and inspiration.

Elsa Steinback, author and artist, provided me with information and consistently encouraged me to continue with the project. She was in the midst of writing a foreword to this book when she passed away in November 1996.

Evans and Frances Herman played an extremely important role in the publication of this book. It was Evans who devised the layout of the chapters and who was instrumental in culling the photographs from a wide variety of sources. I shall be forever grateful to him for his advice and support from the start to finish of this book.

There is no way that I can adequately express my appreciation to Ginger Henry for her dedication to this book. I gave her the substance of the various chapters and she gave each chapter the polish needed. When Ginger and I began our collaboration, Bob Rosen described us as a team like Rodgers and Hammerstein, with me providing the words and Ginger setting them to music. Ginger's enthusiasm and devotion was a continuous inspiration to me. No other person contributed more time and effort to this book; in fact, without Ginger, there would be no book. It was she who convinced *The Chronicle* editor, Mark Frost, to serialize the chapters in his paper, giving the book invaluable pre-publication publicity. And it was she who sent the manuscript to our publishers, Wray and Loni Rominger, of Purple Mountain Press, and convinced them to publish it.

Last but not least, my wife Betty, to whom I dedicate this book, and to my daughters, Gail Street and Janie Weller. Betty was a tremendous source of inspiration. It was she who urged me to continue writing when I was ready to abandon the idea. And it was she who shared 38 years with me on Glen Island, observing the daily occurrences in a ranger's life. During our early years she also performed the duties of a campsite ranger, issuing camping permits, answering the telephone and driving the boat when camper emergencies occurred. She was also the campers' friend, supplying them with various items that they had forgotten to bring along, such as matches, aspirin, first aid needs, and the like. She refrigerated their perishables until the iceman made his rounds and even boarded pets when campers were suddenly called away by an emergency. What more can I say but that she truly was the ideal campsite ranger's wife. And now, in our retirement, she remains the perfect wife.

In addition, I would like to thank all of the individuals listed below, who provided me with valuable information and support:

Claire and Dick Bartlett	Sam Hoopes
Pat Babe	Richard Kober
Joan Baldwin	Tom LaGoy
Megan Baker and the	Lake George Association
Bolton Free Library	Ernie Lantiegne
David Boyd	Robert McIntosh
Betty and Louis Brandt	Ray Supply
Bob Brewer	Photography Department
William Brown	Steve Reynolds
J. Buckley Bryan Jr.	Nancy and Dusty Rhodes
John Brynes	Bob Rostetter
John Byrnes	Wyman Russell
William Busch	LeRoy Ryder
Dr. Leonard Busman	Fenton Sabo Sr.
Henry Caldwell	Harold Shippey
Ted Caldwell	Kathleen Simmes
Chapman Historical Museum	Chester Sims
Thomas Conerty	Steve Soroka
Crandall Public Library	Sally Knapp Sprole
Frank Dagles	Patti Steele
Shirley Dean	Ralph Stiles
Dick Dean	John Stiles Jr.
Todd DeGarmo	Trees (Things Adirondack)
Robert Edwards	Curtis Truax Jr.
Marvin Eger	Harold Tucker
Doug Ferguson	Crosswell Tuttle
Gardner Finley	Esko Virta
Sherwood Finley	Biffy Weller
Mark Frost and *The Chronicle*	Clifton West
Sam Frost	James White
Bob Gates	William White and the
David Geffen	Adirondack Research Library

And special thanks to Jean Rikhoff, author and novelist, for her professional help in seeing this book through publication.

Foreword

ELSA STEINBACK

Lake George is one of the most beautiful bodies of water in the world. It is dotted with islands—rocky, heavily forested and lovely bits of land. Until the late nineteenth century the state had paid little attention to these islands, even selling some of them. As more and more hardy souls began to pack their equipment into canoes or rowboats and venture out to the islands to set up vacation camps, however, the state began to take more notice of the treasures within its bounds. Eventually the need was recognized to establish a small force of rangers to ensure that the wild beauty of the islands would be preserved. From 1941 to 1983, Frank Leonbruno was one of these rangers.

Many of the campers of today have been coming to Lake George for decades. They all have fond memories. They remember their treks to Glen Island—to pick up mail or groceries—as special events. And they remember one individual in particular—Frank Leonbruno. Perhaps Frank's role can best be described as that of host, devoted to the care of his beloved islands and to the well being of their many occupants. During his long tenure as head ranger, Frank took the time to get to know the campers and many of the neighborhood visitors to Glen Island. Over the years he developed lifelong friendships and enjoyed watching more than one generation of several families gratefully appreciate his exceptionally competent oversight of their favorite vacation spots.

In this book, Frank shares his personal memories of these campers and their adventures. Some will make you laugh, while others could bring a tear to your eye. In addition to his extensive research and his own wealth of memories, Frank also relied for his information on owners of the private islands and Bolton old-timers who have been keen observers of the lake, its islands, and its visitors over the years.

With its anecdotes, memories and historical fact, the book is a love story, reflecting Frank's deep passion for the lake and its islands, which began when he first arrived in Bolton as a CCC employee in the 1930s and which continued to grow over the next half century. Frank exhibits a burning desire to protect the object of his affection. He stresses that an equilibrium must be attained between the legitimate requirements of recreational users and the need to preserve the islands. This was his constant goal throughout his years of public service, a goal in which he was often frustrated but which he never abandoned.

It is to be hoped that in the future the delicate but so necessary balance between man and nature will continue to be in the hands of someone as caring as Frank Leonbruno!

Edited from Elsa Steinback's notes for the foreword of this book. Elsa's notes were interrupted by her sudden death on Thanksgiving Day 1996.

Frank Leonbruno and Elsa Steinback, July 1995, at Elsa's Shelving Rock home.

Photo: Ginger Henry

INTRODUCTION

PETER A. A. BERLE

Lake George is one of those places that remains etched in one's memory. The steep wooded slopes that rise up from the rocky shoreline and the islands scattered throughout its entire length are highlighted by clear blue water. Located within New York State's Adirondack Park, much of the land surrounding the lake, and more than three quarters of the 172 islands, are owned by the state. For a nominal fee, one can rent a campsite on a Lake George island. This offers an outdoor experience that will match anything the Rockefellers and Vanderbilts achieved when they bought thousands of Adirondack acres and built their Great Camps at the turn of the century.

Frank Leonbruno was the forest ranger in charge of state operations at Lake George for 42 years. As such, he was one of those special stewards of land who cared for our public property as though it were his own. He took delight in the thrill and adventure that the lake and its islands gave generations of campers. Each visitor enriched the stories that Frank Leonbruno recounts in his memories and reflections.

The Adirondack Great Camps all had cadres of caretakers who looked after the properties and the families of the patrician owners. In many cases the owners and staff regarded themselves as part of a big extended family. As a public steward, Frank Leonbruno's family was all of us who camped on the islands. He watched children grow up and return with children of their own. When the kids got scrapes, bruises, and chills, Frank attended to them. When people abused those precious islands Frank felt pain.

He served at a time when views about the Adirondacks and how they should be maintained were undergoing considerable change. In 1942, when he started his career, it was commonplace for a family to

11

rent a "tent platform" on a multi-year basis. These platforms began to look more and more like houses, with permanent furniture and fixtures.

By the 1970s, state policy changed. Private tent platforms were no longer permitted, and many who thought they had a special claim on some particular site found their platforms being demolished. Also, in response to increasing development pressure on private lands within the park, the state enacted a master land-use plan in 1972. It prescribed building density and other environmental controls on all privately held real estate.

Some Adirondack residents bitterly resented what they considered a violation of their private property rights. Threats of violence aimed at all state employees were not uncommon. An intruder was apprehended one night in the headquarters of the Adirondack Park Agency, the organization that had been established to administer the land-use plan. He was wearing a ski mask and was about to set the place on fire with a can of gasoline. Throughout this critical time, one state employee who retained the respect of everyone was Frank Leonbruno.

Thirty-two miles in length, Lake George has served as a travel corridor from the Hudson Valley to the Saint Lawrence through linkage with Lake Champlain. Throughout the French and Indian Wars, makeshift navies in the summers and men traversing the ice in winter sought to control the lake. At issue were the spheres of influence of Britain and France. Later, during the American Revolution, the Lake George islands were fought over by American and British troops in skirmishes that led up to the battle for Fort Ticonderoga. Frank provides a unique catalogue and account of the islands throughout the grand sweep of American history.

My own experiences on the islands are of little historical significance. But they have a special meaning to me in my personal diary of the Adirondack Park. The park is different from most American parks in that almost half the land is privately owned. About a hundred villages and hamlets are within its boundaries. Representing a district in Manhattan, I served in the New York State Assembly when consideration of legislation to enact the land-use plan and establish the

Park Agency was on the calendar. I had been designated leader of the floor debate in favor of the legislation. Glenn Harris, a lifetime resident of the Adirondacks who had served in the legislature for many, many years, was the leader of the opposition forces.

(In the previous three winters, I had participated in the annual Rogers Rangers Run, which was a cross-country ski trek over the ice covering the entire 32-mile length of the lake. While the event was not billed as a race, the dozen or so of us in the front of the pack spared no effort to finish first. During the two previous years, I had been able to come out on top in part as a result of the Lake George islands. In both years, a headwind blasted down the length of the lake, making cross-country skiing a real test of endurance. I found that instead of taking the most direct route, it was much faster to run in the lee of the next island down the lake. This provided some protection from the wind.)

The floor debate on the Adirondack legislation was scheduled for the week after the ski event. Filled with the insufferable arrogance that often afflicts elected office holders, and spurred by my confidence in the island strategy for skiing Lake George, I issued Assemblyman Harris a challenge. Instead of duking it out on the floor of the Assembly, why not determine the outcome of the Adirondack legislation depending on which of us completed the ski trek first? I offered to give Glenn a five-minute head start for each year his age was greater than mine, and another five minutes for each year of legislative seniority that he held. I noted that this seemed more than fair since he was a red-blooded Adirondacker from the North Country and I was a dissipated Democrat from New York City.

While the challenge received considerable press attention, Glenn, who was not a cross-country skier and whose girth was beginning to show the effect of many years of sitting in his legislative chamber seat, was not amused. Nevertheless the legislation did pass with a coalition of city Democrats and moderate Republicans. Many legislators had been urged to take strong action to protect the Adirondack Park by constituents who cherished their experiences on the Lake George islands.

The Lake George islands and all public lands in the Adirondack Park are protected as forever wild by the New York State Constitution. As such, they will forever enrich the lives of those who celebrate natural beauty. But even wild lands require loving stewardship. Frank Leonbruno provided that for over four decades. His work enriched the lives of thousands of folk who learned to share his view that Lake George is one of the most beautiful bodies of water on earth.

—October 1997

Peter A. A. Berle is director and host of "The Environment Show" on National Public Radio, past president of the National Audubon Society, and former commissioner of the New York State Department of Environmental Conservation.

LAKE GEORGE REFLECTIONS

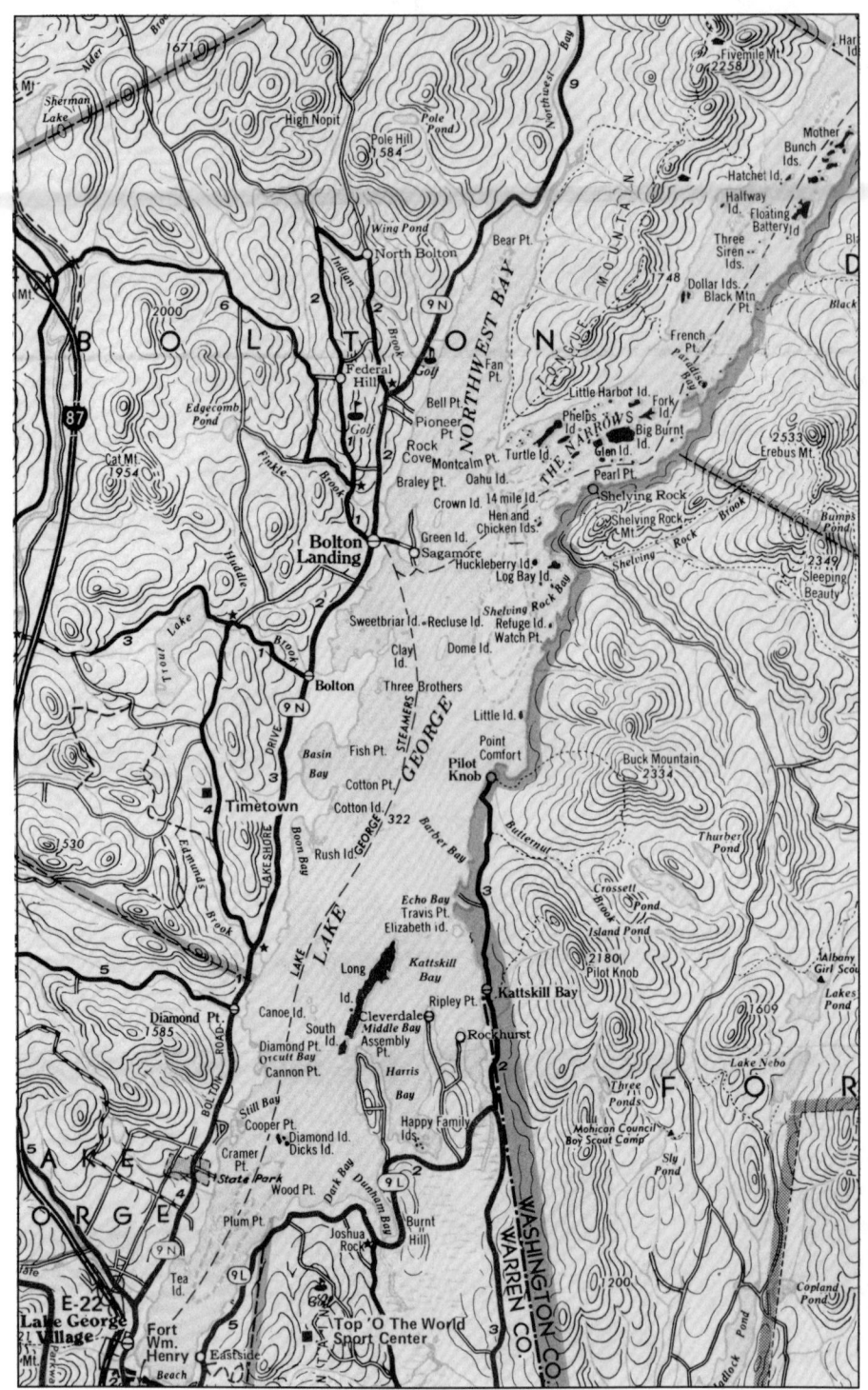

LAKE GEORGE SOUTH

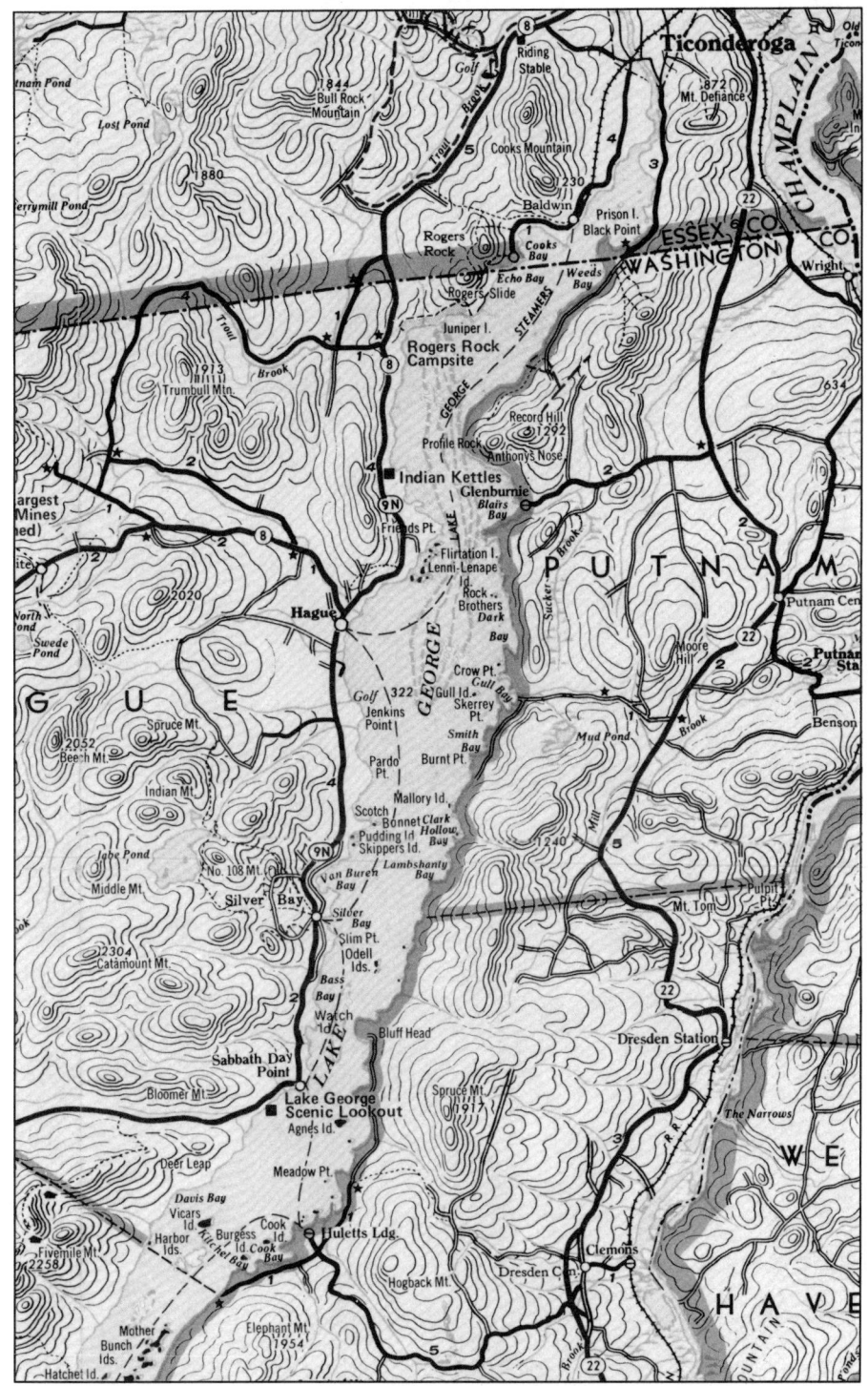

LAKE GEORGE NORTH

Lake George is without comparison, the most beautiful water I ever saw.

Thomas Jefferson
LETTER TO HIS DAUGHTER, MAY 1791

LAKE GEORGE

ITS CHARACTERISTICS, TOWNSHIPS, ISLANDS, AND ITS BEAUTY

GLACIAL MOVEMENTS resulted in the birth of a new lake of unsurpassed natural beauty, extending for 32 miles on a northeasterly to southwesterly axis, enclosed on both sides by high rugged mountains. Lake George, which is nearly three miles at its widest point and has depths of nearly 200 feet, covers a surface of 44.44 square miles. The islands make up 409.2 acres of this, leaving a water surface of 43.8 square miles, or about 28,000 acres. The Lake George watershed encompasses 264 square miles. The shoreline of Lake George measures 176 miles, of which 20 miles are state owned. If the island shorelines are included along with the main shore, then well over half of Lake George's shoreline lies within the Town of Bolton.

Three counties—Warren, Washington, and Essex—as well as one village—Lake George Village—and eight towns border Lake George. The towns, clockwise from the lake's south end, are Lake George, Bolton, Hague, Ticonderoga, Putnam, Dresden, Fort Ann and Queensbury. Over 90 percent of the lake's water is in Warren County, while less than 10 percent is in Essex County. Washington County has no water, just shoreline to the high water mark. Over 75 percent of the lake's waters are in the towns of Bolton and Hague. Bolton's Northwest Bay contains more water than all of Essex County's portion of Lake George.

The lake, which flows from south to north, is 323 feet above sea level and 221 feet above Lake Champlain. The widest point of Lake George, just under three miles, stretches from the mouth of Northwest Bay on the west shore (just north of Crown Island) to Shelving Rock Bay on the east shore.

North of Bolton Landing, Tongue Mountain thrusts its tip out from the west shore. This slender part of the lake, dotted with islands, is appropriately called the Narrows. The southern part of the lake stretches over six miles, from Lake George Village to the southern extremity of Tongue Mountain. The average width here is about two and a half miles. After passing through the Narrows, the lake winds gently north like a river, covering a distance of about 23 miles before reaching the natural dam in Ticonderoga. This part of the lake has a fairly uniform width of approximately one mile. The widest part of open waters is in the Town of Hague, stretching from the town dock across to Dark Bay on the east shore.

PROBING THE DEPTHS

Three very deep and widely separated basins were revealed in surveys made by Seneca Ray Stoddard from 1906 to 1908 and in *A Biological Survey of Lake George* published by the state in 1922. The deepest of the three basins, the central basin, lies fairly close to the east shore, north of Point Comfort. It extends from a point opposite Buck Mountain north to Fourteen Mile Island just offshore from Shelving Rock Mountain. The deepest sounding—187 feet—was made about a quarter mile west of a point known as the Calf's Pen and on a line with the southern end of Dome Island. The Calf's Pen is located on the east side of the lake, about a quarter mile north of Phelps Island.

A second basin, long and narrow, is located close to Anthony's Nose on the east shore near the northern end of the lake. Stoddard's survey revealed a depth of 175 feet. Here, just as in the central basin, the shore's steep mountain slopes continue down under the water.

The smallest and southernmost basin is located in the middle of the lake, opposite Plum Point, about two miles north of Lake George Village. This basin has a depth of 109 feet at its deepest point.

HITTING ROCK BOTTOM

A rocky section of the lake known as the Fields, covering approximately 12 acres, is the largest area of offshore shallow waters. Located in the Narrows, it is bordered to the southwest by Hermit Island and to the southeast by Watch Island. Various maps and navigation aids place this area off limits for purposes of navigation. A small boat with shallow draft could navigate through a small channel between Watch Island and Hermit Island *if*—and I emphasize if—the pilot of the craft is either very skilled or just plain lucky.

During the 42 years that I worked for the state, I recorded numerous accidents in the Fields involving outboards, inboards, and even cabin cruisers whose skippers failed in their attempts to navigate these waters. Fortunately, the boats never sunk, but many were grounded. Damage often was severe, ranging from broken propellers, drive shafts, and rudders, all the way to gaping holes in the boats themselves.

The Fields is a favorite playground for scavengers who delight in wading into the shallow waters to salvage rudders, propeller blades, and shafts, as well as to examine the scratches, gouges, and grooves on the rocks and boulders of the Fields.

Back in the days before long-term island camping was prohibited, I received an unusual request from a man who had set up camp for the summer on Hermit Island. He asked for a permit to operate a seasonal

A casualty of the Fields.   *Photo: Frank Leonbruno*

marina on the island to provide service to boat operators who proved inexperienced in navigating the Fields. Because state law prohibits any commercial activity on Forest Preserve land, the request was, of course, denied.

A second area of shallow waters in the lake is known as the Coop, or the College Group, and is composed of nine unnamed islands. Located west of Big Burnt Island and southwest of the two Gourd Islands, this area has also been the scene of numerous boating accidents. A particularly dangerous channel—one that has been successfully navigated by few, if any, boaters—is that between Gourd Island and a small unnamed island just to the west.

Still another area of shallow waters is that known as the Three Sirens and One Tree (or Fish) Islands. These four islands are located about a half mile northwest of Black Mountain Point, southwest of Floating Battery Island and east of Halfway Island. They are surrounded by waters dangerously dotted with a myriad of rocks, shoals, and reefs.

BENEATH THE SURFACE

Another unique characteristic of Lake George is its bed, which incidentally is owned by the state and falls under the jurisdiction of the Office of General Services. The irregularity of this bed was caused by preglacial movements, and later by the force of the glacier which passed through this area. The glacier left deposits in just the right places to obstruct both the old channels so that the beds of two adjacent rivers flowing in opposite directions were joined to form the bed of Lake George.

The uneven bed of the lake repeats in miniature the broken contours of the surrounding mountains. In fact, if the irregularities of the lake's bed could be photographed it would reveal an amazing similarity to the mountain ranges surrounding the lake. Ridges of rock at or just below the water's surface constitute the lake's reefs.

Even today, scuba divers are still discovering artifacts from the various wars fought on Lake George. These relics include arrowheads, spearheads, rusted cannons, musket balls, firearms, coins and even bateaux. The remains of what was probably an eighteenth-century gunboat are still visible on the bottom of the lake near Floating Battery Island.

Sunken boats (some by choice, some by accident), as well as various parts such as motors, anchors, bow lights, rudders, and flag poles are scattered about the bottom of Lake George. In 1821, Lake George's first steamboat, the *James Caldwell*, burned and sank at its pier in the town of Caldwell (now Lake George Village). The *Scioto*, a 75-foot-long boat with a 12-foot beam, was said to have been purposely sunk in the area of Canoe Island in the late 1940s. The remains of two other passenger steamboats—the *John Jay* and the *Minne-Ha-Ha*—can be clearly seen from the lake's surface. The *John Jay* burned and sank on July 29, 1856, killing six of the 80 passengers on board. Its remains lie in shallow water just off of Calamity Rock, south of Temple Knoll Island in Hague. The *Minne-Ha-Ha*, whose engine was salvaged from the *John* Jay, was launched the next spring. It carried passengers on the lake for the next 20 years until it was taken out of service. Thereafter, the ship was permanently docked in the small bay at Black Mountain Point, serving as a dining room and additional guest rooms for the Horicon Pavilion. Today, huge timbers and parts of the keel and frames of the *Minne-Ha-Ha* lie at the bottom of the bay. In 1901, the original *Ticonderoga* burned and sank near Hawkeye Point at the entrance to Heart Bay at the northern end of the lake.

Seven 30-foot bateaux warships, dating from 1758, rest on the bottom of the lake, near the east shore's Wiawaka Holiday House. This site, known as the Wiawaka Bateaux Site, was listed on the State and National Registers of Historic Sites in 1992.

The remains of a tractor trailer lie on the bottom of the lake near the lookout on the north side of Tongue Mountain. The truck is just one of many which over the years have lost control on this extremely steep segment of Route 9N.

A variety of unusual items rest on the lake's bottom, including ice tongs, ice chisels, fishing tackle, lures, and heavy lead sinkers. Oak logs, lost during the years of log rafting prior to 1900, can still be found in various areas of the lake. The lake's bottom is an ideal hunting ground for driftwood collectors, and well as for collectors of unusual rocks and stones.

In 1966, several of my colleagues at the DEC and I salvaged a number of the oak logs and transported them to a saw mill owned by William Nadeau. Nadeau sawed the logs into various lengths and widths, and we used the lumber to repair our state-owned boats. This wood, which had been under water for over 60 years, seemed to be as good as any recently harvested oak lumber. Some of this same oak lumber may still be in use today at the New York State Green Island Maintenance Center.

Many quartz crystals have been found in the area surrounding Diamond Island. These unique transparent crystals, described by historians as "six-sided prisms," have a perfect form.

Beer cans, bottles, shopping carts, discarded household items, and supplies from the old hotels are just a few of the "treasures" found by the crew organized for the Lake George Association's clean-up days on the lake throughout the 1960s and early 1970s.

THE BOTTOM LINE

During my years of service, I was sometimes called upon to assist in the installation of telephone and electrical power lines in the lake. These lines run, for example, from Diamond Point to Little Canoe Island, as well as from the northwest side of Cleverdale to the east side of Long Island. There also is a submarine cable for telephones which runs from the east side of Green Island over to Fourteen Mile Island and then on to the Knapp property on the east shore. In October 1995, new telephone lines were installed from Green Island to Oahu Island, continuing across to Fourteen Mile Island and the Knapp property. There are also electrical and telephone lines from the Knapp property to Glen Island, as well as from Oahu Island to cottages along the Tongue Mountain shoreline. A telephone and electrical cable also runs from Narrow Island to Fredericks Point at Huletts Landing on the east shore. To avoid getting their wires crossed, fishermen would be wise to find out the exact locations of these and other underground cables before tossing in their lines.

HYPOLIMNION

Hypolimnion is, according to the Rensselaer Polytechnic Institute's Fresh Water Institute, headquartered in Bolton Landing, water at the bottom of the lake that is held in place by a dense heavy layer of water just above it. The hypolimnion layer contains nutrients released by decaying matter on the bottom of the lake. Because the bacteria in the decaying matter uses up the oxygen in the surrounding water, the dissolved oxygen levels are typically low. The greater the amount of decaying matter, the lower the oxygen levels.

The most recent findings of tests carried out on the hypolimnion layer in the southern basin of the lake reveal three significant changes: lower oxygen levels, a greater abundance of plankton, and higher levels of phosphorus. These facts could spell trouble because salmon and other marine life cannot live in waters where there is too little dissolved oxygen.

There is another important point to understand about the hypolimnion. In the spring and in the fall, when the upper waters reach a certain temperature, a "turnover" occurs. This means that the water at the bottom, with all its impurities, is mixed with the water above—the water in which people swim, the water which they drink. It is here, too, that the algae feed.

Though we may not as yet be able to detect any major changes in these surface waters, the changes in the hypolimnion should be taken as warning signs. Despite the fact that water quality in the open expanses of the lake remains good, it is by no means excellent, and there is a good probability that it will continue to deteriorate, particularly if storm runoff is not controlled. Studies of the lake reveal that phosphorous is the chief culprit in the deterioration of the lake. We on Lake George are extremely fortunate in having the RPI Fresh Water Institute here to monitor water quality and keep us informed about other environmental changes affecting the lake.

A prime example of environmental change is the invasion of milfoil, an aquatic weed that has taken root in Lake George in recent years. It was first discovered at three sites in the lake in 1985, although some property owners claim that they had noticed it in previous years.

The Lake George Association was the first group actively to lobby the Department of Environmental Conservation, the Lake George Park Commission, the Adirondack Park Agency, the Warren County Board of Supervisors, state legislators, and the public at large about the dangers of this weed. Once introduced into a body of water, milfoil multiplies rapidly until boating and swimming become unpleasant, if not impossible. The Fresh Water Institute, active in monitoring the spread of milfoil, has found it in pockets throughout the entire lake. New York is the only state which has refused to approve Sonar, a chemical that has proved useful in battling milfoil. Recently, the state agreed to allow limited testing of the chemical in Lake George.

HISTORY

I could not recount the history of Lake George without first mentioning the lake's various names. The Native American tribes who first inhabited this beautiful lake called it by two different names. The Iroquois named it *An-Di-A-Ta-Roc-Te*, which means "the lake that shuts itself in," while, for a short time, another Indian tribe named it *Caniad-Eri-Oit*, meaning "tail of the lake."

On May 30, 1646, the French priest Father Isaac Jogues christened it Lac du St. Sacrement, a name which stuck for 109 years until, in 1755, General William Johnson renamed it Lake George in honor of King George II of England. During the nineteenth century, James Fenimore Cooper, author of the novel *The Last of the Mohicans*, tried unsuccessfully to rename the lake Horicon. In the preface to his 1851 novel, Cooper said that the French name was too complicated, the American name too commonplace, and the Indian names too difficult to pronounce.

The suggestion has been made by various writers that the name of Lake George should be changed. I, for one, firmly believe that there is no more reason to change the name of this lake than there is to change the name of its individual islands, a feat which also has been attempted by some.

However, if a change were to be made simply for the sake of change, the lake should bear the name of the first white man ever to lay eyes on it, Father Isaac Jogues, or at least the name which he gave it, Lac du St. Sacrement. But this is all hypothetical, since, in my opinion, this beautiful body of water will forever keep its name of Lake George simply because its millions of admirers would never allow it to be changed.

Many renowned visitors to Lake George have described its great beauty. Thomas Jefferson, who visited here in May 1791 on a fishing trip, wrote the following letter home to his daughter on the bark of a paper birch tree:

> Lake George is, without comparison, the most beautiful water I ever saw; formed by a contour of mountains into a basin thirty-five miles long and from two to four miles broad, finely interspersed with islands, its water limpid as crystal and the mountain sides covered with rich groves of Thuja, silver fir, white pine, aspen and paper birch down to the waters edge, here and there precipices of rock to checker the scene and save it from monotony. An abundance of speckled trout, salmon trout, bass and other fish with which it is stored, have added to our amusements the sport of taking them.

Seneca Ray Stoddard, noted historian and author, referred to Lake George as the "Queen of American Lakes."

The Bolton Landing author Wallace Lamb perhaps said it best: "There is—there could be—only one Lake George."

In closing, let me tell you the story of a lady who spent her summers at Lake George. When she died and went to Heaven, she wandered about the streets of gold there, meeting such famous inhabitants as Saint Paul, Moses, Solomon, Adam and Eve. One day, she met a former acquaintance who had owned a cottage at Roger's Rock in Ticonderoga. "How do you like it here in the Celestial City?" the acquaintance asked. "It's nice," she replied, "but it's not exactly Lake George, is it?"

Dollar Islands, on the west side of Lake George, just north of French Point, and looking south. Dome Island is in the far distance. © *Richard K. Dean*

The Islands
of Lake George

MILLIONS OF YEARS ago, as glaciers pushed through the region, they left in their trail a myriad of islands strung throughout the lake. It is these islands which give Lake George its unique charm, making it one of the most picturesque bodies of water in the world.

Hemmed in on both sides by high forested mountains rising precipitously from the water's edge and dotted with almost 200 wooded islands of varying sizes and shapes, Lake George has rightfully been crowned the "Queen of American Lakes." But without its islands, would the lake still be worthy of that title?

The exact number of islands on Lake George always has been the subject of great debate. New York State Department of Environmental Conservation maps record 172 islands, though only 128 of them have names. Because the various DEC maps have not been revised for several years, however, the island count is only approximate. A new survey would undoubtedly show that some islands have vanished, literally washed away by erosion. Others have been created, also by erosion, as chunks of land have broken off from the mainland and other islands. I have heard some individuals claim that the lake sports 365 islands—one for every day of the year. During leap year, they contend, a 366th mysteriously appears.

Based on the research I have conducted, I believe that the original glacial movement created 250 islands. My belief is based on the existing islands plus the large number of ledge-type reefs located just below the lake's surface. These reefs undoubtedly were once islands, covered with soils and vegetation. Over time, however, erosion wreaked havoc, turning the once-fertile islands into underwater rock ledges.

Historian Wallace Lamb fixed the actual island count somewhere between 220 and 225. In his 1889 book, *Lake George,* Seneca Ray Stoddard reported that his 1880 visual survey of the lake revealed about 220 islands. This count, he pointed out, included every rock around which high water breaks.

Less than 40 years later, however, a 1917 to 1919 survey commissioned by the New York State Conservation Department documented the existence of only 172 islands. The survey was conducted by Albert Davis, R.E. Doherty and Thomas Lee, Jr. A map based on the survey was compiled by Arthur Hopkins and Albert Davis. High water levels, heavy winds, rain, and the push of ice all contribute to the destruction of soil and vegetation on the islands.

Of the 172 islands listed in the state survey, 148 were owned by the state, while 24 were privately owned. In the ensuing years, the state added to its territory by purchasing Turtle, Long, and Speaker Heck Islands. During that time, however, it also lost title to three islands— The Triplets—located on the east shore near Travis Point and Echo Bay. A Conservation Department report of 1922 concluded that these three islands originally had been a part of the mainland prior to the raising of the lake level in about 1800. Because that part of the mainland had been included in a 1774 Royal Patent, the state was precluded from owning them.

In 1942, a committee appointed by the state legislature to study Lake George water conditions listed 200 islands in its inventory. Maps published by the state between 1919 and today differ in the number of islands cited. Some indicate a total of 172 while others show 176 islands. This discrepancy arises from the fact that the Harbor Island group, consisting of five islands, is sometimes counted as one island. In addition, Cooper's Point is sometimes listed as an island, when in fact it is part of the mainland. Until a new survey is conducted of all islands and the term "island" is clearly defined, it will remain impossible to say exactly how many islands actually exist on Lake George.

To satisfy my own curiosity, I recently consulted the assessment rolls of the towns of Bolton, Hague, Lake George, and Ticonderoga in order to establish an inventory of Lake George islands. According to these figures, the total island count is 178: Bolton has 106 state-owned and 25 privately owned islands; Hague has 45 state-owned and no privately owned islands; Lake George has only one island, the privately owned Tea Island; and Ticonderoga also has just one island in its jurisdiction, namely the state-owned Prison Island.

Over the past 75 years, the islands which have been lost to erosion include Willow, Manhattan, Ranger Island Shoal, Arrow, and a number of unnamed islands. To the casual observer, the existing islands might appear unchanging over time. But in recent years erosion has reduced the size of many of them, namely the Happy Family group, Prison, Lenni-Lenape, Asas, Ship, Pudding, Rush, Goose, One Tree, Loon, Mallory, Skippers Jib, and Scotch Bonnet.

Erosion remains a very viable threat and will continue to be so as long as Mother Nature is around. However, it is my hope that erosion control measures will be set up in the near future by the state in order to protect the islands. These measures consist of protective stone walls (rip-rapping) built around the endangered islands.

To many residents, campers, and tourists, the islands of Lake George represent a special treasure. We owe a debt of gratitude to the state for its early recognition of the need of its residents for recreational areas and for its recognition of the unique experience made possible through island camping. Lake George was one of the first areas developed by the state for island camping. Now, as we approach the end of the century, it is up the state to ensure that the delicate balance is preserved between conservation and recreational use of the islands.

Regardless of whether they number 172, 176, or 178, each and every one of the Lake George islands is special to me as well as to thousands of other people. And I sincerely hope that action will be taken before one single island more is lost to erosion.

Not all the islands on Lake George have chapters devoted to them. The islands described here are listed as the lake flows—from south to north. When islands are approximately on the same latitude they are listed from west to east. Refer to the maps of Lake George on pages 16–17.

31

TEA ISLAND

T EA ISLAND is the most southerly island on Lake George, located just off the west shore about a mile and a quarter north of Lake George Village. It is one of just a handful of islands which is not within the municipal boundary of the town of Bolton.

New York State sold Tea Island to Egbert J. Gale on April 15, 1859, for $10. However, records indicate that as early as 1772 Tea Island was included in a British land patent granted to Frederick Shonnard. Apparently, the state gained ownership sometime thereafter. Tea Island was just one of the islands which the state sold into private hands between the years 1855 to 1871.

Seneca Ray Stoddard, noted photographer, historian, Adirondack guide, and author of travel guides, called Tea Island a "perfect little gem" in his 1882 description of it. It is from Stoddard that we learn how the island presumably got its name. "On the north side," he wrote, "stands the ruins of what was once a stone summer house. It is said that in 1828 a tea house was kept here, to accommodate visitors, from which circumstance it is mistily presumed came the name. It is also reported that, before the eastern rim caved in, the hole went clear through to China, forming an underground route, whereby honest importers could get their teas without the ordinary expense of buying a custom house officer."

Stoddard, as well as other historians, wrote of gold and valuables buried on the island by Abercromby during the French and Indian Wars in mid-century. According to one report, Abercromby buried chests containing the payroll for his 12,000 troops. Throughout time, treasure seekers have combed the island looking for the fortune, but to no avail. What they did find, however, was a large number of arrowheads, a clear sign of Indian activity here.

During the era between 1855 and 1895, guests from the Fort William Henry Hotel, built at the southern tip of the lake in 1854, would row out to Tea Island. Here they would disembark, often with a picnic lunch, to spend a relaxing afternoon on this tranquil island. Egbert Gale's brother, Daniel Gale, was the manager and later owner of the Fort William Henry Hotel.

One of the guests during these years was a 12-year-old boy who was later to become president of the United States. This boy kept a diary of his travels which indicate that he, his younger brother, and his cousin rowed to Tea Island during a stay at the Fort William Henry Hotel. The entry in his diary was dated August 2, 1871, and the boys' names were recorded as Teedie, Elliot and James. Teedie later became known as Teddy. And his family name, of course, was Roosevelt.

In 1872, Gale sold Tea Island to René and Harriet Nivert of Paris, France. Since that time, the island has changed hands many times, sometimes being sold to family members for $1. In 1934, it was purchased by Charles Tuttle, a New York City attorney, counsel to the Lake George Association, and member of the Lake George Park Commission. Upon his death in 1971, Tea Island was bequeathed to his three daughters, Evelyn T. Horne, Charlotte T. Walkup, and Jasmine T. Bryant. Today it is still owned by the heirs of the Tuttle family.

I was on this island only once, back in about 1960, shortly after ice-out. Ed Lamb, a DEC employee, and I were making the first trip of the season out to Glen Island when our state boat, the *Banshee*, broke down. The prevailing wind carried us close to Tea Island, and we paddled ashore to wait for assistance. While we were waiting, we had the opportunity to view the remains of the old tea house. After much white flag waving, we finally attracted the attention of another boater who towed us back to Hall's Marina, which is about a mile from Tea Island, on the east shore of the lake.

My quest was to set foot on every island on Lake George at least once. I was delighted when circumstances caused us to land here since Tea Island was one of the few islands which had evaded me in my mission.

DIAMOND ISLAND

DIAMOND ISLAND is a small, state-owned island about three miles from the southern tip of the lake, about midway between the eastern and western shores.

The name is derived from the quartz crystals found on the island. As early as 1820, a family inhabited the island, making its living from the sale of minerals mined here. The stones were described as "six-sided prisms which are hardly surpassed by any in the world for transparency and perfection of form."

Today, this island is a haven for scuba divers who are rewarded not only by the occasional crystal found on the lake's bottom but also by the sunken boats in this area.

One of these boats is a 45-foot gasoline launch built in 1906 which went down east of Diamond Island in the 1930s under unknown circumstances. This boat, named *The Forward* and formerly owned by the Bixby family of Bolton Landing, is now a New York State Submerged Heritage Preserve.

East of Diamond Island are two small islands, one unnamed and one named Dicks (also formerly called Dix).

According to historian Wallace Lamb, General James Abercromby used this island as an encampment for about 400 men during the French and Indian War. At that time, it was considerably larger than it is today. As is the case with so many of the Lake George islands, erosion has taken its toll on Diamond Island.

During the American Revolution, General John Burgoyne fortified this island for use as a supply base after his capture of Ticonderoga in 1777. He left Captain Thomas Aubrey in command as he marched south toward Saratoga.

At the same time, the American Colonel John Brown, with 500 troops, led a surprise attack on Fort Ticonderoga, capturing a large number of boats and a few cannon. He then headed down the lake to attack Diamond Island. In this effort, however, he was less successful, as Aubrey's gunboats drove the Americans north toward Van Wormer Bay (now called Warner Bay). In desperation, the Americans burned all but two of their boats before retreating over the mountain, leaving the British to retrieve the remaining boats and the cannon. Historians differ in their opinions of whether the burning of the boats occurred in Dunham's Bay, which is directly across from Diamond Island, or Warner Bay.

Diamond Island has had a variety of owners over the past century and a half. In 1859, Egbert J. Gale purchased it from the state for $10. In 1892, owner Dr. Arthur R. Paine sent a letter to *The Lake George Mirror* asking the editor to draw attention to the fact that Diamond Island "is one of the few islands in Lake George that does not belong to the state, and is not public, but private property." Dr. Paine pointed out that the announcement was made necessary by the fact that parties had been camping there without permission, defacing the property.

The island was also owned at one time by Mrs. Katrina Trask, wife of Spencer Trask, renowned New York financier. Edward Morse Shepard, upon learning that Mrs. Trask had fallen in love with the island, purchased it and gave the deed to Mr. Trask so that he could present it to his wife. Mrs. Trask turned it into a shrine for peace in honor of various Native American tribes who came to the island to smoke the pipe of peace. The Trasks built a dock and pavilion here so that visitors could enjoy the beauty of the island, and erected a four-sided stone pillar known as the "Peace Stone." The stone, which was given to Mrs. Trask by Shepard, bears several inscriptions, one of which is "Peace, here the conqueror of many wars 1666-1777."

At the base of the stone monument, another inscription recounts the lake's early military history:

> French armys passed this island under Courcelles 1666. St.
> Helene 1690. Manteth 1693. Vaudreuil 1746. Dieskau 1755
> Montcalm 1757–1758. Colonist–English Army under

Diamond Island Monument. *Photo by Dick Swire*

Abercrombie and Howe. After defeat 400 here encamped . . .
island called "Diamond" . . . 1777 two companies 47th British
Infantry, Colonel Montressor and Capt. Aubrey fortified and
September 24th defeated Americans twenty three days before
British surrender at Saratoga.

Mrs. Trask had the following Biblical verse inscribed on a bronze
plaque on the stone: "He maketh wars to cease in all the world. He
breaketh the bow and knappeth the spear in sunder and burneth the
chariots in the fire. . . . Be still then and know that I am God."

In her will, Mrs. Trask left Diamond Island to the American Scenic
and Historic Preservation Society. However, the public in general
apparently did not appreciate this gracious gift as the premises were
neither cared for nor maintained.

In 1951, after three years of effort by the Lake George Association,
the state of New York accepted Diamond Island as a gift from the
society.

It was at that point that I was instructed by my immediate superior,
Clarence Badman, Lake George Park Superintendent, to clean up the
island, which had become unsightly. Our garbage barge was used to
haul away rusted tin cans, paper, bottles, and other debris. We also put
a new roof on the pavilion, and built a new dock and an outhouse.
This latter was important since there was no small amount of human
waste on the island. In 1952, the New York State Conservation
Department officially declared the island a day-use area.

Today this island can accommodate several parties of day users,
with dock space for six boats, picnic tables, fireplaces, toilets, and a
large picnic shelter. Many visitors come to the island to see the stone
monument on its north end.

With title to the island now vested with the state, we can rest
assured that visitors can continue to enjoy this historic and beautiful
island and that Mrs. Trask's kindness and generosity will be
remembered.

Before closing this chapter, I would like to recount another tale
concerning Diamond Island. According to historian Max W. Reid's
book, *Lake George and Lake Champlain*, it was the habitat of a large

number of rattlesnakes. In fact, many inhabitants of the region were afraid to go near the island for fear of these snakes.

It is also reported that a hog farmer, Jost Storm, passed by Diamond Island when he was transporting seven hogs by boat to a farmer on the other side of the lake. Smelling the rattlesnakes, the hogs rushed to the side of the boat, capsizing it. The animals swam immediately to the island, where they disappeared into the brush. The men managed to keep the boat afloat and paddled to shore.

Winter was fast approaching. Storm, who fell ill, made no effort to capture the hogs, assuming that the rattlesnakes would kill them. Three years later, his son Jim, along with a friend, donned high boots and thick gloves, picked up their shotguns and clubs, and set out to visit the island. They ventured cautiously onto the island, keeping their eyes peeled for the rattlers. But, after scouting the entire island, they discovered only one rattlesnake. The hogs, on the other hand, far from having been annihilated, had multiplied into a herd of 16 fattened beasts.

The hogs were taken ashore and butchered. Every one of them was full of rattlesnakes. According to an eyewitness, some of the snakes were still alive. As Reid wrote, "There was another queer thing about these hogs. One of them had a litter shortly afterwards, and sir, every one of the piglets had a rattle on the end of its tail."

One man, it is said, made sausage of the pork. He reported, "It tasted alright, but I had to watch it while frying, because it tried to crawl out of the frying pan."

I leave it to the reader to believe Reid's tale or not. Some may call it fancy, legend, or myth without basis in fact. Nevertheless, this story does illustrate one point which may be of interest to the reader who is not familiar with rattlesnakes. A rattlesnake bite will have no ill effect unless the venom enters the bloodstream. A hog's heavy layer of fat beneath its skin keeps the venom from the fang from entering its blood.

THE CANOE ISLANDS

THESE THREE islands, located between Diamond Point and Long
Island, were formerly known as Seven Mile Islands or Three Sisters
Islands. They were sold by the state in 1861 to John W. Edwards for
$10. In 1880, Edwards sold them for $400 to N. H. Bishop, Lucien
Wulsin, and Judge Nicholas Longworth. Longworth, who was
married to the daughter of Teddy Roosevelt, was speaker of the House
of Representatives from 1925 to 1931.

The current name derives from the fact that the 23 organizing
members of the American Canoe Association held their first meeting
here on August 3, 1880.

The largest island is now owned by William and Jane Busch. Mr.
Busch, owner of Canoe Island Lodge on the mainland, is a former
chairman of the Lake George Park Commission. The island, with its
natural beach, serves as an excursion point for guests of the lodge,
providing an excellent spot for swimming, picnics, and parties. It has
no buildings on it. William and Jane Busch told me in October 1993
that they plan to keep the island free of any structures forever, though
they want to ensure that guests of Canoe Island Lodge will always be
able to use it for excursions. If they ever sell the lodge, they plan to
impose restrictions to ensure that the island remains in its natural state.

The most northerly of the three islands, Little Canoe, was purchased
in 1971 by Frederic and Louise Davidson. They commissioned Olaf
Ronning of Bolton Landing to build them a home and guest house on
the island. An underwater power cable, which cost $8,000 to install, as
well as an underwater telephone line brought some of the conveniences
of mainland living to the island.

Tragedy, however, struck on August 15, 1981, when the guest house was completely destroyed by fire, resulting in the death of a two-year-old child whose family was staying on the island at the time. A Lake George Park Commission patrol boat and the Warren County Sheriff's boat were first on the scene. When I heard the report on the fire department scanner, I rushed to Green Island, where *Henry's Dipper*, the large DEC utility barge normally used for collecting sewage from the islands, already was loaded with fire equipment and about six firefighters. Twenty-nine volunteers from the Bolton Fire Department responded, along with firefighters from Lake George. We used *Henry's Dipper* to ferry firemen and equipment to the island from the Diamond Point dock. Unfortunately, we were unable to save the child, who died before our arrival. Robert Moon of the Warren County arson team determined that the fire was started by a towel draped over a lamp in the toddler's room.

After rebuilding the house, the Davidsons sold the island to Bob and Ada Bailey for $600,000.

The third and smallest island, called Baby Canoe Island, measures less than 1,000 square feet in size. It never has been developed, but has changed hands several times. At one point, Warren County even owned it, having repossessed it for failure to pay taxes. Today it is owned by Sam Frost of Lake George.

One of the former owners gave the Lake George American Legion post permission to raffle the island as a fund raiser. Of course, the idea of owning a Lake George island aroused a great deal of interest and many raffle tickets were sold. The winners of the raffle turned out to be an unsuspecting Canadian couple who happened to be passing through town. After learning that their $2 raffle ticket had won, they asked William Busch to take them out by boat to see their prize. Upon realizing that the island was too small to build a house on, however, they decided they were not at all interested in keeping it.

Sam Frost offered the couple $1,000 for the island. Seeing a chance to make a $998 profit on their $2 investment, the Canadians quickly accepted the offer. In the past, Sam occasionally picnicked on the island, but he has not made any use of it since the early 1980s. He should be commended for purchasing this island for the sole purpose of preserving it as a complement to the beauty of the other two islands.

LONG AND SOUTH ISLANDS
(NOW SPEAKER HECK ISLAND)

LONG ISLAND, also once known as North Island, is the largest island on Lake George, measuring over 97 acres in size. It is more than one mile long and has a shoreline of nearly three miles.

Although history does not record any battles on Long Island during the French and Indian Wars, it was used for military encampments. On one occasion, 500 to 600 Frenchmen and Indians who were part of Vaudreuil's forces camped here. General Montcalm moored his boat at the island in 1757. Later, Abercromby stationed 400 Englishmen on Long Island, along with an equal number on Diamond Island. In 1758, on a bitter cold March night, Robert Rogers and 358 of his Rangers and Mohawk followers camped here on their return from a scouting expedition to Ticonderoga, at the north end of the lake. It was so cold that nearly two-thirds of the party suffered frostbite. In the 1970s, a perfect arrowhead was found on the southern part of the island by the caretaker's assistant, testimony to the presence of Native Americans.

On July 4, 1770, the island (Long Island and South Island were considered to be one island) was deeded by King George to a pair of British soldiers, George Underwood and James McGowan, for their services to the crown during the French and Indian Wars. However, at the end of the Revolutionary War, these two Tories abandoned their holdings and fled to Canada.

The first person who cleared the island and attempted to farm it was Jonathan Irish in the 1830s. Irish later sold it to Amos Hendryx, who built a house on the island. Amos was the grandfather of Benjamin Hendryx of the Farm to Market Road. It is said that he cut large quantities of hay on the island, transporting it to the mainland over the ice each winter.

On May 10, 1871, Dr. Drurie Stanford purchased the island from
Hendryx for $5,000, a sizable sum in those days. He was the son of
Dr. S. T. W. Stanford who had made his fortune in the patent
medicine business in Long Island City. His patent was for Stanford's
Liver Invigorator, a red liquid containing no small quantity of
alcohol. Although it seems somewhat ironic to me that alcohol could
be considered invigorating for the liver, it was apparently well
enough received to make Stanford a wealthy man. In 1946, during
our first cleanup of the island, I found a bottle of Stanford's Liver
Invigorator. I suppose that even today, if you knew where to dig, you
might still unearth a bottle or two of this medicine somewhere on
Long Island.

The Stanfords built a three-story home and a bicycle path which
ran completely around the island. They also built many benches and
rustic summer structures at various places along this path. The small
offshore islands were referred to as the Stanford Islands. Dr. Stanford
once told Howard Mason that he was so grateful to Amos Hendryx
for selling him the island that he never passed Hendryx's grave in the
Bay Road Cemetery in Glens Falls without raising his hat. The
Stanfords became gentlemen farmers, building several small buildings,
a large barn, chicken coop, and a separate rooming house for the
farmhands.

In 1891, the state attempted to claim ownership of South Island. It
contended that it was a separate island, divided from Long Island by a
small channel of water. However, the Jackson map 2 of 1757 and the
Robert Harpus map of 1765 reveal that Long and South Islands were
actually one and that erosion had caused their separation. The case
went to court, with Dr. Stanford emerging the victor. His argument,
which apparently swayed the court in his favor, was that when he
bought the island, he had carried his bride from one island to the
other without getting his feet wet.

Dr. Stanford died in 1926. His widow Addie died in 1930, leaving
the property to her two daughters. The large main house burned in
the mid-1930s, along with the family's treasured possessions,
including four pianos, an organ, and a variety of antiques collected

over the 74-year era. One of the Stanford daughters, Jane McRae Dube, remained on the island with her husband, Thomas N. Dube, until about 1938. Over the course of time, the island and its buildings had slowly begun to deteriorate and the Dubes found themselves in arrears in their county, town, and school taxes. They moved to the mainland on Assembly Point and put the island up for sale, leaving a caretaker in charge. This caretaker, whose name was Ramsey, fell through the ice during the winter of 1943 and drowned.

Around 1942, it was rumored that a lumber company was interested in purchasing Long Island for its lumber. The state had been interested in the island for many years, hoping to turn it into a public campsite. In 1945, Mrs. Dube and her sister, Mrs. Balmer, finally sold Long Island and South Island to the state for $30,000. It should be noted that the Lake George Association was instrumental in bringing about the state's acquisition of both of these islands.

In 1946, I worked with other Conservation Department employees to demolish the existing buildings, including chicken coops, a cow barn, the caretaker's house, the blacksmith shop, and the boathouse. While scouting the island, we found the remains of a sugar house, a large sap pan, and a grove of maple trees at the north end of the island, indicating that the Stanfords had made maple syrup during their years on the island. One building, a studio, was left standing, but was torn down in 1949 under the supervision of Bernard Ramsey (no relation to the caretaker who drowned), Park Superintendent of Lake George. In 1947, a campsite caretaker was hired to issue permits for the island.

Ramsey also supervised the construction of the ranger station on Long Island in the late 1940s and early 1950s. Under his guidance, Conservation Department employees built 86 campsites and a large day-use area. Because the docking space proved to be inadequate for a day-use area, this was later converted to campsites.

On August 14, 1976, Long Island was the site of a wedding ceremony when Jack Brynes, Long Island campsite ranger from 1970 to 1978, tied the knot on the main lawn, near the circular flower garden that he had planted the year before.

South Island is located approximately 300 feet south of Long Island. At the time that this island was sold to the state, several old camps, shanties, and one or two cottages were located here. One of these camps was moved by its owner to the east side of Assembly Point in 1946. In order to move the camp in one piece, the owner cut down several trees on the island, an illegal act for which he paid a stiff fine.

During the same time that Long Island was being returned to its natural state, employees of the Conservation Department also demolished all of the remaining buildings on South Island. The island was later developed into campsites and eventually converted solely to a picnic island.

In 1968, at the urging of the Lake George Association, South Island was renamed Speaker Heck Island in honor of Oswald Heck, long-time speaker of the New York State Assembly and an advocate of legislation to protect Lake George. A plaque signifying this honor is found on a picnic shelter at the south end of the island.

Today, the island has the capacity of accommodate up to 360 people. It has picnic tables and charcoal burners, three picnic shelters, 12 privies, and dockage for 52 boats.

Long Island, without a doubt, has more species of trees than any other island on the lake. These include white and red cedar, various maples, red and white oak, shag-bark hickory, Norway and white pine, hemlock, beech, honey locust, and mulberry trees, among others. Several apple trees grow near where the ranger's cabin now stands. In the early 1970s, we started an arboretum in the field south of the ranger's cabin, planting a variety of small seedlings. Many of these today have grown into lovely trees.

A blowdown occurred in 1950, severely damaging the east side of the island. Most of the trees which were affected were white cedar and white pine. Work crews worked throughout the entire winter of 1950–51 clearing the downed timber. We transported all of the salvageable trees across the ice to Assembly Point and then trucked them to the Lake George Maintenance Center near Fort George Park. In the spring, the logs were rafted and then towed to the

Diamond Point dock from where they were trucked to a sawmill. The cedar trees were used to make picnic tables while the pine logs were turned into lumber.

Because of its variety of vegetation, Long Island has an interesting wildlife population. Animals such as raccoons, squirrels, chipmunks, otter, and even a few mink have been observed. As many as four deer have been sighted here in a group, tame enough to let people come within 10 yards before ambling off. Ranger LeRoy Ryder, who was stationed on the island from 1966 to 1968, remembers repeatedly seeing two deer—a six- and an eight-pointer—throughout the 1966 camping season. Today, Ryder is my successor as supervisor of Lake George Island Operations for the state.

Speaker Heck Island and Long Island are still assessed as one island. They carry the highest assessment of any state island on Lake George, at just under $11 million.

RUSH ISLAND

RUSH ISLAND is a state-owned island located near the west shore, at the entrance to Boon Bay in the town of Bolton. Just how this island got its name is unknown. However, I believe that it may have come from the fact that rush—a grass which thrives in wet areas—was once present on the island. Or it may derive from the tiny island's exposure to the prevailing southeast winds, causing the water to "rush by."

The shores of Boon Bay are lined with vacation cabins. The owners of these cabins and their guests always delighted in swimming out to this nearby island. There they could fish, swim, work on their tan, or simply enjoy a few hours of peace and quiet.

But Rush Island has, over the years, not been treated kindly by Old Man Winter and his Ice Corps. In 1963, insult was added to injury when the island was ravaged by human vandals who cut some of the few trees which had managed to gain a foothold. The damage was reported by Joseph Schweins, owner of Diamond Village Motel at that time, who asked the Lake George Association what could be done to help reverse the rapid deterioration of the island. The LGA immediately contacted Bernard Ramsey, park superintendent at the Conservation Department. Ramsey, in turn, asked me to take immediate action. After inspecting the damage, I dispatched a crew to work on the island. Using stones brought in on a state barge as well as stones found at the site, the men rip-rapped the island. When this was completed, they brought in fill and sod to protect the island from future perils of man and nature.

The very next day, we received a phone call from the Horst H. Schroeder family, landscapers and owners of another motel on Boon Bay, who wanted permission to plant two small willow trees on Rush

Rush Island.   *Photo by Frank Leonbruno*

Island. The willows were an ideal choice since their root system provides excellent protection against erosion. Today, one of the willows has grown to become one of the island's largest trees, easily spotted by motorists passing by on Route 9N. A lovely 25- to 30-foot soft maple and a cedar tree add to the beauty of this tiny island.

Rush Island is an excellent indicator of ice-out. In the spring, when the lake begins to honeycomb, the interested observer should watch this island. When it becomes covered with what appears to be snow—actually honeycombed ice—it is a pretty sure bet that this section of the lake will be free of ice within two or three days.

In May 1996, LeRoy Ryder (my successor at DEC) and I inspected what remains of the severely eroded island. Rush is in dire need of restoration as Mother Nature continues to wreak havoc. If action is not taken soon, this island will probably disappear. Hopefully public interest will become strong enough to force the state to recognize the gravity of the problem and take appropriate steps to prevent the loss of Rush Island.

Yes, Rush Island, you are small and you have been badly mistreated. But to both year-round and summer residents of Boon Bay, you loom as their favorite. In fact, one group of Boon Bay property owners calls itself the Rush Island Association, guaranteeing that, regardless of the island's future, its name will always remain a part of Boon Bay.

47

THREE BROTHER ISLANDS

THIS GROUP of three islands just off the lake's western shore in Bolton, near Homer Point, has had several names over the years, including Three Brothers Islands, Three Sisters Islands and Triuna Island.

New York State sold these islands for $10 on April 15, 1859, to Egbert Gale, the son of a prominent Lake George family. In the 1880s, Louis H. Meyer, the owner of Alma Farm, seven miles north of Bolton, purchased the islands. Although Alma Farm was a year-round working farm, the Meyers only lived there during the summer months. While at the farm, they often made excursions to the islands, but never built any permanent structures on them.

Wall Street financier Spencer Trask and his wife Katrina spent the summer of 1906 on Clay Island, where they rented a cottage. It was during this stay that the Trasks decided that Lake George would make an ideal summer home. Clay Island, however, was too large for their tastes. They were looking for a small, secluded place where they could escape the endless rounds of entertainment which had become a part of their life at Yaddo, their Saratoga estate.

The Trasks began their search for a site where they could build a modest home. Katrina urged Spencer to inquire about purchasing the three small rocky islands located just south of Clay Island and listed on old maps as Three Brother. Mr. Trask had not given these islands serious consideration, thinking that they were too small for his purposes. Mrs. Trask, however, saw the possibility of building Venetian-style bridges between the islands in order to utilize all the available space. She envisioned the northernmost island as housing the kitchen, laundry, and household servant quarters, with a Gothic arch and belfry setting the service area off from the rest of the property. Her plan also included a long vista and promenade under two colonnaded bridges, stretching across the middle island and on to the third island. On this third and southernmost island the Trasks envisioned their own residence.

In spite of his initial doubts about the project, Mr. Trask was awed by his wife's enthusiasm and went to work to enlarge and develop the islands. He purchased scores of old stone fences from local farmers, who were amazed and gratified that the "rock crop" brought in more income that year than the rest of their harvest combined. As soon as the lake froze that winter, these stones, along with other rocks and soil from the surrounding mountains, were transported across the ice and carefully placed between and on the islands.

Once the islands were joined, Mrs. Trask renamed them Triuna Island, meaning three-in-one. The rocks and stone served as the foundation for the connecting bridges. These structures, as well as the buildings on the islands, all in Norman Gothic architecture, were

Three Brother Islands. (Dome Island is in the background)   © *Richard K. Dean*

49

stained in earth tones. A bell cast at the Meneely Bell Company in Troy was placed in the belfry. Its soft chimes welcomed many visitors to the island over the years. Dedicated by Bishop Done of Albany, the bell has the following inscription:

> Sprinkle with holy sounds the air,
> O blessed bell: ring out all care,
> Ring in true love and peace and rest
> To this trine island of the blest.

During the summer of 1909, the Trasks were called away from Lake George to attend to business matters. A national economic crisis was putting a serious strain on Mr. Trask's finances. In December of that year, Mr. Trask was seriously injured in a train accident. He was traveling in his private railroad car, attached to the end of a passenger train, when it was hit by a freight train near Croton-on-Hudson. Although none of the other passengers on the train was hurt, Mr. Trask was so severely injured that he died shortly thereafter, on December 31. Mr. Trask's sudden and untimely death had a dire effect on Mrs. Trask's vision for an endowed artist's retreat at Yaddo and Triuna. With the reduction in her financial resources, she was forced to make major modifications in her plan.

In the summer of 1913, through an employee's carelessness, fire reduced most of the north island's buildings to ashes, charring the surrounding trees. The Trasks' 55-foot launch *Pocahontas*, three motor boats, five rowboats, docks, boathouses, a storage shed, informal dining room, servant quarters, kitchen, laundry, and workshops were all destroyed in the fire. Mrs. Trask, who was seriously ill at the time, was transported from the islands in a rescue boat. From her sickbed at Yaddo, she supervised the reconstruction of the damaged buildings. But she was never to visit Triuna again.

On February 5, 1921, Katrina Trask married George Foster Peabody, a friend and colleague of her late husband. Peabody owned a "cottage" on the Bolton Road, a house which later became the home of Adolf Ochs, publisher of *The New York Times*. However, the marriage was short lived. Katrina died 11 months later, on January 8, 1922, never having left the confines of Yaddo during that period. In her will, she left the use of the West House at Yaddo and five acres of grounds surrounding it to Peabody, who remained in possession until his death in 1938. The will also specified that Yaddo and Triuna were to be utilized as a retreat for musicians, writers and artists.

During the late 1930s, Yaddo's board of directors determined that the islands were too expensive to operate as part of the artist colony. Despite the fact that a number of renowned and creative individuals had taken advantage of the island retreat, including John Cheever, who spent several summers there, the board decided to sell Triuna and use the limited remaining resources for Yaddo. Bob Gates of Bolton was hired to remove the furnishings and other valuables from the islands. Some of these were taken to Yaddo while the others were probably sold.

William and Virginia Speed of Louisville, Kentucky, purchased the islands in 1940, modernizing and refurbishing the main house according to their own tastes. They restored the original name to the islands—Three Brother. The Speeds, who owned a number of homes, usually spent only one month of the year on the islands. During the summers of World War II, however, they often did not come to Lake George at all.

On Labor Day weekend of 1950, the property was sold at public auction to Max Swire for $38,100. The family consisted of seven brothers and two sisters, who originally came from Albany. Max believed that by having a place at Lake George, the close family ties would continue to the following generations. They divided the houses, studios, caretakers cottages, and two archway apartments among themselves. Each of the nine families have separate quarters. The Swire family was no stranger to Lake George. Many of them had camped on the state-owned islands as early as 1915. During my time working for DEC, I issued permits to many Swires, including their children, who camped at various times on Big Burnt, Ranger, Juanita, and Fork Islands.

Shortly after the Swire family purchased Three Brother Islands, Isadore Swire and Celia Swire Caplan, both former island campers, took me on the grand tour of their prized new possession. Today, the only surviving member of the original nine siblings is Max Swire, who turned 93 on December 23, 1995. I was privileged during the summer of 1995 to spend a delightful afternoon with him on Three Brother Islands, sharing our reminiscences of days gone by on the lake and its islands.

Dick Swire, Max's son, now lives on the island year round with his wife, Pat. It is the only Lake George island with year-round residents. As the Swires can attest, island life is not only often somewhat inconvenient during the winter months, but sometimes can be downright dangerous. Having a safe means of transportation to the mainland, which is about 900 feet away, can be a problem both in early winter during freeze-up and in early spring when the ice is melting. During these times, they use a canoe as a sled to skim along the ice, propelling it with ski poles if the ice is thick enough to hold them or with paddles if the ice breaks beneath them. In this manner, they make daily trips to the mainland to get their mail and newspapers and to do errands. Pressure ridges, a dangerous condition caused by the ice's movement, often form in the ice near the Swires' house, and have been known to rise up higher than the windows in their house.

The Swires' love for the islands and for the lake itself is so intense that they are willing to put up with the perils of winter in exchange for the privilege of this unique year-round island life. Their skill and ingenuity in coming up with solutions to the problems which Mother Nature presents are admirable.

DOME ISLAND

DOME ISLAND, located midway between the east and west shores and about nine miles north of the southern tip of the lake, is the centerpiece of Lake George's scenic setting.

It is the highest island on the lake, rising 76 feet above the lake's surface. The origin of its name is clear. Seneca Ray Stoddard once described it as having "the appearance of a huge emerald dome, somewhat flattened, but bearing enough of the appearance to justify the name."

Dome Island is a glacial moraine—an accumulation of earth and stones deposited by a glacier. With its unspoiled beauty, the island probably looks the same today as it did a thousand years ago. Its heavily wooded landscape, composed primarily of hemlock, beech, and red oak, provides a habitat to a wide variety of animal life.

Like so many of the Lake George Islands, Dome played a role in the military campaigns of the French and Indian Wars. The elevation of the island made it an ideal place for English scouts to spy on the Indians encamped among the islands to the north. It is reported that Colonel Israel Putnam left some of his troops on the island while he went to inform General Webb of the presence of Indians on the islands near Northwest Bay and the Narrows.

On October 11, 1856, the state of New York sold Dome Island to William Smith of Albany for $50. Smith sold it one year later to Pliny Sexton, a chancellor of Union College in Schenectady, for $100. Sexton encouraged students at the college to take advantage of Dome Island. They enjoyed picnicking there, as well as canoeing and rowing in the surrounding waters. A 40-foot Union College banner, decorated in garnet and white, was hung on the island when the students or others from the college were there.

Two paintings of Dome Island as seen from Sloop Island were executed by John Frederick Kensett in 1869. One hangs in the Metropolitan Museum of Art; the other is in the Corcoran Gallery in Washington, D.C.

Today, thanks to the efforts of John Apperson, who purchased the island on September 1, 1939, from Mrs. Katherine McCaddon, Dome is ensured of remaining forever wild. Apperson, noted Lake George conservationist, donated the island to the Northeastern New York Chapter of the Nature Conservancy in 1956, making it the chapter's first preserve. Apperson's decision to place the island in the Conservancy's hands was the best thing that could have happened to Dome. The soil conditions on the island are extremely fragile, and its steep banks of sand and gravel would easily crumble if trampled upon by visitors. Any damage to the soil holding the native woodland herbs and shrubs would subject the banks to severe erosion.

Dome Island is not open to the general public. Individuals or groups can, however, arrange for guided tours by calling the Nature Conservancy in Troy. William White, of Schenectady and Bolton, has been the unofficial caretaker of Dome Island for the Conservancy since 1956. Much like Apperson, he has devoted considerable time and energy over the years to the preservation and betterment of Dome Island and Lake George. White's interest in Dome Island began during his childhood when he accompanied Apperson on trips to the island. Though Apperson never stayed on the island, White remembers he always brought along a can of baked beans just in case he got stuck there and couldn't make it back to shore.

On September 16, 1995, I was honored to be part of a Dome Island preservation effort organized by the late Chester Sims of Bolton. With the help of Bolton teachers Ted Caldwell and John and Debbie Gaddy and a group of 17 Bolton students, a stretch of about 30 feet of severely eroded shoreline on the northeast end of the island was rip-rapped. The students, who were members of the Bolton Outing Club, formed a kind of bucket brigade, passing the stones down the line and putting them in place. I was very proud of this group of teenagers whose interest in our environment was so strong that they sacrificed their free time to assist in the rip-rap project.

During a slide presentation by Sims that morning and a walking tour of the island in the afternoon, the students learned about John Apperson, the history of Dome, and the need to protect it. Sims, who died in early 1996, was extremely interested in the preservation of Lake George, and Dome Island in particular.

Dome Island is indeed a great landmark. We owe John Apperson a debt of gratitude for his foresight and generosity in ensuring that one island on Lake George will remain unspoiled for future generations to enjoy.

On May 7, 1970, tragedy struck near Dome Island. Forest ranger James White of Bolton Landing called me to request boat transportation. He said that he had been alerted by a DEC helicopter pilot that a DEC boat which had been stocking rainbow trout had capsized approximately 200 feet off the northeast end of Dome Island. We were told that two DEC fish and wildlife technicians were on board and that only one of them had made it ashore to Dome Island.

Jumping into the state boat *Nancy*, we raced toward Dome Island. The lake was very rough that day, with winds out of the northwest. As we neared the island, we spotted John Pasko waving for assistance. He told us that the 16-foot, 25-horsepower aluminum boat in which he and Arnold Morehouse had been riding had swamped and that he had last seen Morehouse clinging to two life cushions in the 47° water. After searching for some time, we found the overturned boat drifting about a mile southeast of Dome Island. But there was no sign of Arnie.

We took Pasko to Chic's Marine in Bolton, where members of the Bolton Rescue Squad treated him for hypothermia. The DEC and Warren County Sheriff's Department organized an immediate and extensive search for Morehouse, utilizing a helicopter and numerous boats. However, the search proved futile. Recovery operations continued for several days as scuba divers searched the entire area while other rescue personnel dragged the bottom of the lake. Many dedicated law enforcement employees and volunteers unselfishly gave of their time to assist in the search. But it was not until July 2 that a Lake George Park Commission patrolman located the body. The drowning was indeed a great tragedy on Lake George.

Sweetbriar Island

SWEETBRIAR ISLAND, less than a half acre in size, is located just off the west shore, opposite the Algonquin Restaurant in Bolton Landing, at the entrance to Huddle Bay.

In the nineteenth century, the island was leased from the state by William A. Wait, a cashier at Glens Falls National Bank, who built a narrow, three-story home on it. However, when the state began enforcing its 1885 law prohibiting any permanent structures on state Forest Preserve lands—which included the state-owned islands—the house was moved to the mainland. A photo of the original house hangs on the wall of the late Chester Sims' home just south of Sweetbriar in Huddle Bay.

How Sweetbriar Island derived its name is unknown. I assume that a number of sweetbriar bushes, a favorite old-fashioned rose with fragrant foliage, formerly grew on the island. Perhaps the Wait family planted these bushes during their residence there. The name first appeared on the chart of Lake George prepared by R. J. Brown in 1899. However, prior to that, Seneca Ray Stoddard recorded it as Huckleberry Island on his 1880 map, probably owing to a growth of huckleberry bushes there. And even earlier, in an 1876 atlas of Warren County, it was named for still another berry when it was assigned the name Whortleberry Island.

The island was originally designated by the state as a camping and day-use area. In the early 1930s, state forest rangers constructed a typical Adirondack-style log lean-to. Over the next 20 years, the lean-to was utilized by campers and day visitors until it was finally torn down in 1954. In the late 1950s the island's status was changed to day use only. By the 1960s the island was showing signs of overuse and the

DEC closed it to the public. The footings for the fireplaces and cement pads which anchored the dock can still be seen on the island.

Prior to the ban by public use, the island had become a haven for some of the local second home owners, particularly after 10 PM, when the island was officially closed for the night. Not ones to be deterred by the posting of day-use hours, boisterous groups turned the island into a "night use" area, staging their beer blasts to the accompaniment of loud music which carried all the way to the Huddle Bay area and nearby islands, namely Leontine, Hiawatha, and Clay.

I recollect receiving numerous phone calls from property owners on the nearby shore as well as from a cabin-colony owner, all of whom were disturbed by the noise coming both from the island and from the constant boat traffic ferrying passengers back and forth.

On several occasions we were forced to contact the state police, meeting them on shore and transporting them with our boat, the *Banshee*, out to Sweetbriar Island, where as many as 30 young men and ladies were partying into the wee hours.

The party goers never gave us a hard time and readily vacated the island after we talked to them. I'm certain that any one of this group who reads this chapter will surely recall with a smile, "I was one of those rascals." Today, most of them are fine upstanding citizens. Some of them still reside in Bolton or return for visits. At least one of those "rascals" is now an attorney. There is also a school teacher or two among them, at least one town councilman and some successful entrepreneurs. One of these entrepreneurs requested, before his untimely death, that his ashes be spread on Sweetbriar. His family followed his wishes so that his resting place is on the island he loved so much.

Another incident which occurred on this island is a prime example of public abuse of state land. During Labor Day weekend of 1957 a group of rambunctious and disobedient youngsters, celebrating the end of summer, took over the island for their celebrations. Although no complaints were made at the time of the party, the aftermath was devastating. Lakeshore property owners reported beer cans floating in Huddle Bay, and the island itself was strewn with garbage, paper, cans, and bottles. The outhouse and one of the picnic tables were burned almost to ashes.

But not all users of Sweetbriar have had only destruction on their minds. This island possesses the distinction of being the only state-owned island on Lake George to have had its own Christmas tree. On a cold winter night shortly before Christmas in 1992, Bolton residents Dick Fahey, Doug Houghton, Henry Caldwell, and Zandy Gabriels were warming themselves in the Algonquin Restaurant, getting into the Christmas spirit, when they decided that the lake could use a bit of added spirit. Gazing out the window at Sweetbriar, the group came up with the idea of decorating a cedar tree on the northwest end of that island. Gathering up a few strings of lights, along with a gasoline-powered generator, they climbed into their 14-foot aluminum outboard and ventured out to the island to decorate the tree. In the days thereafter, equipped with a can of gasoline, they returned to the island just before dark to refill the generator and light the tree. For 10 days, and for about 12 hours each day, Sweetbriar's Christmas tree was lit, to the wonder and delight of all those on the nearby shore—townspeople and tourists alike.

Sweetbriar is very popular with amateur photographers on the lookout for a scenic Lake George landscape. Its proximity to shore, its tranquil sylvan beauty, and its lovely mountain backdrop of Buck, Little Buck, and Pilot Knob Mountains make this island an ideal motif for camera bugs.

At this writing, the future use of Sweetbriar is uncertain. It will depend on DEC's philosophy and the environmental condition of the island. But, if it were to be put back into use, my recommendation would be for camping only, limited to no more than two persons at a time. I would be sorry to see it converted to a day-use island, which would result in more individuals using it and more wear and tear on its fragile ecology.

Yes, Sweetbriar, the town of Bolton has assessed your value at just under $100,000. But the rascals, the campers, and day users of yesteryear would undoubtedly say, "Your value is far more. No mere mortal can assess the worth of our memories of you, for they are truly priceless."

RECLUSE ISLAND

ACCORDING TO legend, the Jesuit missionary Père St. Bernard found refuge on this island after escaping from his Indian captors. During his lonely one-year stay on the island, St. Bernard recorded his experiences and tribulations on the pages of his prayer book. Hidden under a rock, the diary remained intact and was later discovered by early visitors to the island. Perhaps this explains the name Recluse.

During the second half of the nineteenth century, the island's name was sometimes recorded as Picknick (or Picnic) and sometimes as Recluse. When Egbert J. Gale bought it from the state in 1859 for $10, the deed listed it as Picnic Island. Toward the end of the century, however, the name Picnic gradually fell out of use.

In 1864, Gale sold the island for $50. The buyer was Rufus Wattles, vice commander of the Mohican Boat Club, who constructed a home there. Named The Hermitage, it was the first residence to be built on a Lake George island. In the summer of 1868, the island made headlines in the New York City papers when it became the subject of a hoax. The papers reported that the island had sunk 80 feet below the water's surface. Curiosity seekers, rushing to the scene to see the oddity for themselves, quickly realized that they were the victims of a practical joke. Perhaps the rumor originated from some poor misguided soul who believed that the added weight of the house would sink the island.

The island changed hands several times over the next decades. Wattles sold it in 1870 to Volney Green, but bought it back from him just a year later. It was sold to Even Barton in 1876, and to Pliny T. Sexton, chancellor of the University of the State of New York, in

1883. In 1924, Sexton sold it to his daughter, Lucy Giese. Because the original Colonial-style house had burned down in 1914, Lucy's husband Hans commissioned the present house, the architecture of which is Moorish Revival style. However, a tragedy occurred during construction of the house. Lucy was on an extended tour of Europe with her family when she became ill and died. Grief stricken, Sexton wired home to have the house put on the market immediately, never returning to the island to see the finished product. Today it is rumored that Lucy's ghost inhabits the house.

Kenneth Reynolds, whose family had been dispossessed by the state in 1917 from an island in the Narrows, was on a fishing trip when he saw the "For Sale" sign on Recluse Island. Rushing back to Bolton, he bought it on the spot. Reynolds was a noted architect from Albany, the designer of many race tracks throughout the country, including those at Saratoga and Monticello.

There was once what historians described as a graceful bridge connecting Recluse to a smaller island, formerly known as Sloop Island. A rustic summer cottage was built on the northern tip of Sloop, a name which derived from the island's similarity to a small sailing vessel with a single mast.

Today, Sloop is known as Little Recluse. Although the town of Bolton's assessment rolls do not list this island as state land, DEC maps record it as belonging to the state. For many years we placed "State Land" signs on this little island until we finally decided that, since the ownership could not be determined, we would remove the signs. Since the Reynolds family claims ownership of Little Recluse and the state has taken no action to dispute this, it seems that the legal status is in a state of limbo. Perhaps the costs of taking this issue to court would be greater than the actual value of the island.

In 1958, Bolton town historian Ruth Seaman wrote that Indian relics such as arrowheads, hatchets, stone knives, and fragments of material from which they were made were frequently found on the island in earlier times. The earthworks on the north and west sides of the island have been attributed to General James Abercromby, whose armies fought throughout this region during the French and Indian War.

In the mid-1930s, while digging a foundation for the ice house (which is still on the island today), the Reynolds family unearthed a cannon. The curator at Fort Ticonderoga examined it and determined that it was a 1790 naval gun, probably used in the War of 1812. The Reynolds family placed the cannon on the northeast point of the island where it remained on display until it was stolen around 1973.

Stephen Reynolds, who lives on the island today, and I both think we know who the cannon thief is, but unfortunately we have no definitive proof. Although the Reynolds family has combed the entire property with metal detectors looking for additional artifacts, none has turned up.

At least three generations of the Reynolds family have been the proud owners of this lovely and historic island. Today it is owned by Stephen and his two nephews, William and Thomas Reynolds. I owe Stephen, an Albany attorney, a debt of gratitude for providing me with much of the information regarding this island's unique history.

Stephen recalls that when his grandmother, who had a strong attachment to the lake, passed away in 1942, her dying words were, "Oh dear, can't I have another summer on the island?" In fact, her request may have been granted. Since that time, strange occurrences have periodically been reported on the island. Stephen remembers that on several occasions his hair would suddenly stand on end when he walked under the staircase in the house.

The strangest event, however, was in 1974, when Stephen brought a friend and her three-year-old son to the island for a visit. After disembarking from the boat at the dock, Stephen remembers, he took his guests up to the house and unlocked the front door. He then returned to the boat to fetch the luggage. The child first ran into the front hall, then out of the house and down to the dock, asking Stephen, "Who's the lady?"

Surprised, Stephen asked, "What lady?"

"There's a lady and she's smiling at me," the child replied. He added that the lady was beckoning for him to come up the stairs. When Stephen asked the boy to describe the woman, he gave an exact description of Stephen's grandmother. Although the child could have no way of knowing what the grandmother looked like, his description was exact, Stephen relates. Other guests have also reported seeing the grandmother, usually in the room which was once her bedroom. Stephen emphasizes that he is "not the least bit of a ghost believer." But, he continues, "there's no question that there's something unusual about that island."

REFUGE ISLAND

THIS STATE-OWNED island, slightly more than a half acre in size, is located so close to the eastern shore, near Wyden Point, that navigation between it and the mainland can be risky. Although the island is composed mainly of a solid mass of rock, there is one area with sufficient soil and trees to accommodate a single campsite with a tent platform.

Refuge Island always has been a favorite with the locals, serving as a retreat from the hustle and bustle of Bolton during the busy tourist season. This factor, along with an incident which took place there on a summer day in 1870, led to the island's name.

The incident was recorded by Seneca Ray Stoddard. Erastus Smith, owner of the Kenesaw Hotel on Fourteen Mile Island, had taken a party of guests out in a rowboat, planning to travel up the lake for a picnic. However, while they were out, a severe storm blew up very suddenly, as storms often do on Lake George. When night fell and the party had not returned to the hotel, the other guests grew worried. Venturing out into the dark and stormy night, they positioned themselves on the point, waving lanterns to light the way home. But it was to no avail. The travelers did not return.

It seems that Smith and his party, caught in the storm, had landed on a small island to wait it out. As they huddled together on the island, however, the storm grew worse, and they were forced to resign themselves to the fact that they would have to spend the night there. When morning broke, the storm had passed and Erastus Smith rowed the party—somewhat worse for wear—across the now-still waters back to the hotel. There the adventurers were greeted with cries of great relief from family members and other guests as they related their tale of a long and uncomfortable night on a small island which they promptly christened Refuge.

My only personal recollection of note of this island concerns a huge piece of driftwood which I found there. This oddly shaped piece of wood, measuring about six feet in length, had an amazing resemblance to a shark. I believe that a camper manually shaped a shark's head and jaw from the driftwood. When I first spotted this marine creature it was very close to the shoreline on the northeastern end of the island. Fearful that the shark might take to the waters if the lake level became too high, I removed it to Glen Island, where it became part of a driftwood collection on display there.

GREEN ISLAND

GREEN ISLAND, the second-largest island on Lake George, is unique in many ways. With its 66 acres, it is the largest privately owned island, the only island which is used commercially, and the only one connected to the mainland by a bridge over which cars, trucks, buses, and other motorized vehicles can travel.

The island originally was owned by Jacob and John Vandenburgh. During that time, cattle were driven through the lake each spring and left on the island to graze throughout the summer. In the fall they were brought back to the mainland.

In 1855, the Vandenburghs deeded the island to Ferdinand Theriot and James Buchanan Henry—nephew of and private secretary to President James Buchanan—for $600. Theriot and Henry surveyed the island in 1868, carving it into lots which they divided between themselves. (Ginger Henry, who helped with this book, is the great granddaughter of James Buchanan Henry.)

The Green Island Improvement Corporation, consisting of a group of investors from Philadelphia, purchased the island in 1882 and 1883, paying $10,000 for Theriot's share and $20,000 for Henry's. The original stockholders of the Green Island Improvement Corporation were E. Burgess Warren, William B. Bement, Robert Glendering, and George Burnham.

In 1881, Myron O. Brown began construction of a hotel on Green Island. Brown had been operating the Mohican House on Mohican Point in Bolton under a lease from W. Rodman Winslow. However, when the lease expired Winslow did not renew it, having decided to take possession of the property for himself. He suggested that Brown build a hotel of his own, noting that Green Island would make an ideal site.

During the winter of 1882, a rustic bridge was built linking the island with the mainland. Construction of the hotel was completed the following spring, and it opened its doors on July 1, 1883. The hotel, named Sagamore, was managed by Brown until 1905.

It was a handsome Victorian building with a large porch which wrapped around the first floor. The main entrance faced the lake, with lawns sloping gently down to the water. The huge wood frame structure offered stunning views from all of the guest rooms. Adolph Ochs, publisher of *The New York Times*, and renowned photographer Alfred Stieglitz were among those who visited the hotel under Brown's management. Guests arrived and departed by steamer from Lake George Village, since at that time there was only limited stagecoach transportation between Bolton and Lake George Village. Some of the lumber used in building the hotel also was transported by steamboat to the site.

In 1882, while still proprietor of the Mohican House, Brown convinced the federal government to open a Post Office near the hotel. He named the site Bolton Landing and suggested that Frederick W. Allen be appointed postmaster. Allen served from September 14, 1882, until 1894. At the time the Sagamore Hotel was built Bolton Landing consisted of four residences, one store, and the Baptist church.

The Sagamore could accommodate 300 guests. Room prices ranged between $17.50 and $25.00 per week, while board cost $3.50 to $4.50 for the week. Two of the original stockholders, Warren and Burnham, built private homes on the east side of the island, facing Shelving Rock. Warren's home, which he named Wapanak, is a fortress-like structure resembling a medieval castle.

On June 27, 1893, after 10 years of operation, the hotel was completely destroyed by a fire which, having originated in the laundry room, quickly swept through the building. Fortunately, no one was hurt in the blaze and some of the furnishings were salvaged. This was before the days of the Bolton Fire Department, which was first incorporated 26 years later, in 1919.

The loss was estimated at $200,000, of which only $128,000 was covered by insurance. Nevertheless, the stockholders decided to rebuild immediately.

Mr. John Boulton Simpson of New York City, who had become a stockholder as well as president of Green Island Improvement Corporation, purchased a lot on the south end of the island. There, in 1894, he built a large house which he named Nirvana. In 1930, this house was sold to Karl P. Abbott, who was the manager of the hotel from 1930 until 1945. Louis Brandt purchased it in 1945, using it as his summer residence until his death in March 1994.

The Green Island Improvement Corporation opened the second Sagamore Hotel in the summer of 1894, with Brown remaining as manager. The new hotel was designed to accommodate the same number of guests as its predecessor, but with considerably more amenities. Most of the rooms had private baths. Along with tennis courts, there were row boats, stables for horses, and a building housing a bowling alley. A power plant on the grounds supplied electricity which was used, among other things, to operate the hotel's new elevators. A Western Union office in the new hotel provided telegraph service.

On Easter Sunday of 1914, 20 years after it opened, the second Sagamore was destroyed by fire. Since the hotel was only open during the summer months, there were no guests in the hotel at the time. The loss this time was estimated at $300,000, with $159,000 covered by insurance. The Charles W. Cool Insurance Agency of Glens Falls was the insurer.

After the 1914 fire, Ernest Van Rensselaer Stires and Bolton architect/contractor Robert Rhinelander turned the building housing the bowling alley into a dining room/clubhouse where those who owned private residences on the island could take their meals. That building, still standing today near the tennis courts, is now used for storage.

There were six private homes on the island. Col. T. E. Roessler had a home built on the southwest side of the island, facing south. Today, the Sagamore swimming pool occupies the site where the Roessler house once stood. A rental house was built by the Sagamore Hotel for Bishop

Ernest M. Stires and his family. The Stires family spent three summers in this house before moving to their own home and farm in Northwest Bay. The Judsons then purchased the property from the hotel.

In 1920, Dr. Willy O. Meyer and his wife Lilly built a private home on the island. Situated just north of the Judson house, facing the western shore of the lake, this three-story home was constructed completely by local tradesmen in a period of just six weeks. Dr. Meyer, born in Germany, was a renowned surgeon. It is said that he once performed a secret operation on President Grover Cleveland, removing a malignant tumor from his jaw.

The owners of these homes were deeded the use of all roads "now or hereafter built on the island." Because no cooking was allowed in the private homes, the residents had to take their meals at the hotel. An agreement between the Green Island Improvement Corporation and the private homeowners also stipulated that the corporation would supply each home with ice, water, and electricity, and that all properties had to be maintained in a "park-like" manner, with no fences separating the properties.

In 1923, the third hotel was built on the site of the first two, at a cost of $105,000. It was relatively small, with only about 30 rooms. The driving force behind this endeavor was Dr. William G. Beckers, who had come to the United States from Germany in 1901. He made the decision to build the hotel after gazing for long hours toward Green Island from his mansion, built in 1916 at the south end of Huddle Bay. He noticed that the island was cooled by a constant breeze, making it an ideal site for summer guests.

While searching for a manager for the hotel, Dr. Beckers was introduced through a mutual friend, C. Everett Bacon of Glens Falls and Bolton Landing, to Karl P. Abbott from the Kirkwood Grill in Camden, South Carolina. Abbott, impressed by the beauty of the area but concerned that the hotel was too small to turn a profit, made a sporting proposition to Beckers. He said he would run the hotel for a season; if it was successful and made as much of a profit as the hotel had lost in the preceding year, Beckers would have to increase the number of hotel rooms by 200.

The second Sagamore Hotel, destroyed by fire in 1914.

Beckers accepted the challenge. Abbott brought in a French chef and began a catering service. With this added business, Abbott won his bet, and in October 1929 ground was broken for the necessary additions to the original building. Construction was progressing rapidly, with the framing completed, when suddenly everything was brought to a screeching halt: The stock market had crashed. Beckers, having suffered huge financial losses, was unable to continue with his plans for enlarging the hotel.

It was at this point that William H. Bixby, who had a summer home at Mohican Point in Bolton Landing, decided to purchase the hotel. Although Bixby was from St. Louis, Missouri, his mother, Lillian Tuttle, originally was from Bolton Landing. He had always admired the location of the hotel and, upon hearing of Beckers's difficulties, had shares of the hotel stock transferred to the Essex Investment Company, a privately held corporation owned by the Bixby family. Under the new ownership, work resumed on the expansion. On July 1, 1930, the hotel opened with 164 guests registered for the very first night.

The first season's successful operation earned the Sagamore a splendid reputation as a family hotel. Guests returned year after year. The hotel hired junior and senior hostesses who were responsible for arranging bridge games, tennis matches, and other entertainment for the guests. Tennis, swimming, and dance instructors were also on hand. The guests also were treated to live music for dancing every night in a night club. On the verandah, they could enjoy music at tea time, as well as ballroom dancing demonstrations.

By this time, many of the contractual arrangements between the hotel and the private homes had been abandoned. The hotel was no longer required to furnish the private homes on the island with ice, water, and electricity, and cooking was now permitted in the homes. The hotel, however remained the center of social gatherings for homeowners of Green Island.

For many years, the original stockholders of the Green Island Development Corporation, as well as several other individuals, had been contemplating construction of a golf course. As early as 1914, the *Glen Falls Times* wrote, "[John Boulton] Simpson says golf is the controlling influence these days that makes or breaks the success of every resort property and his company must recognize this fact and equip themselves accordingly if they desire to attract necessary patronage."

In 1928, at a cost of $500,000, a beautiful 18-hole golf course, designed by Donald Ross and said to be one of the 10 most difficult courses in the country, was built on Federal Hill on the mainland, complete with a club house. This privately owned course was open to hotel guests as well as to the public. In 1938, the golf course was sold to the Sagamore. Many of the young men in Bolton worked as caddies here over the years.

The 13 Lake George property owners who had family privileges at the golf course in 1938 were William H. Bixby, William B. Dean, Mrs. S. C. Edgar, Jr., Maurice Hoopes, Leon P. Janinet, Edward Mattes, Frederick MacDonald, William B. Smith, C. Everett Bacon, Peter D. Kiernan, M. L. C. Wilmarth, Jerome G. Meyer. and Warren Neidringhaus. Other local names mentioned in correspondence concerning the golf course are William G. Beckers, Adolph Ochs, I. A. Stevens, Mrs. James R. Knapp, and New York State Senator Frederick W. Kavanaugh as trustees.

The Sagamore Hotel was always bustling with activity. One weekend the hotel would host an A. A. U. swim meet; the very next weekend there might be a P. G. A. golf tournament or a nationally-recognized horse or dog show. For three summers (1934 to 1936), the Gold Cup inboard boat races were held in Bolton Bay in front of the hotel.

During the years of World War II, many changes occurred. People had a different focus to their lives. With many men away in the service, high taxes and the lack of gasoline for trips to Lake George, the hotel began losing money. Many of the large private homes on the lake were not even opened up by their owners during those years. It was definitely not a profitable time for a summer hotel. In 1945, Abbott closed the hotel as usual in the fall. It was his last summer as manager of the Sagamore. (Karl Abbott wrote a book about the Sagamore, entitled *Open for the Season*. A copy can be found in the Bolton Free Library.)

In April 1946, a syndicate headed by Charles Morton, a vice president of the New York Central Railroad, and New York State Senator Elmer F. Quinn from New York City was formed to buy the hotel. Other stockholders were New York City theater owners Harry, William and Louis Brandt, New York City attorney Milton C. Weisman, and dress manufacturer Philip Zahm.

The new syndicate purchased the hotel and golf course. William Dino, who had been manager of the Sand & Surf Club in Palm Beach, was hired as general manager. But by the time the hotel opened in 1946 it was in the hands of Sagolf, a wholly owned subsidiary of Brandt Enterprises. This company owned, in addition to many New York City movie theaters, Arcady children's camp on the shores of northern Lake George and Schroon Manor Hotel, located farther north in the Adirondacks.

Louis Brandt was a man with a mission. He was intent on purchasing the hotel which, just a few years earlier, had discriminated against his family because they were Jewish. Discrimination at hotels

71

and restaurants was not uncommon in the early decades of this century, as many establishments wanted their clientele to reflect management's own religious and cultural values. Brandt, whom I considered to be a friend, made me well aware of the instances of discrimination practiced against his family by the Sagamore Hotel under Abbott's management. Under Brandt, the hotel continued to discriminate, though now it favored rather than rejected Jewish guests.

With his manager, James Fayko, Brandt ran a different type of hotel. It was intended for adults, with many of the guests coming from the world of entertainment. They often were the parents of children attending Camp Arcady. When the outdoor movies offered by the hotel proved unsuccessful, Brandt built a movie theater housing the largest screen outside of New York City. He also added a night club as well as indoor and outdoor swimming pools. For many years, the Sagamore was a thriving resort.

In 1948, Brandt attempted to reinstate the original arrangements with the private home owners. The home owners, however, initiated and won a law suit which ensured them the right to use the roads, large dock, and public parlors at the hotel, while exempting them from the requirement of having to take their meals at the hotel.

At that time, there were only three private homes remaining on the island. These were the homes formerly owned by Meyer, Judson, and Roessler which had been purchased by George O'Connor of Waterford, Peter D. Kiernan of Albany, and William Stoutenburgh of Ridgewood, New Jersey, respectively. Of the other original houses, the Burnham home on the east side of the island had been purchased by the Sagamore and later torn down, the Warren house (often referred to as "the castle") had been purchased by the Sagamore to house hotel staff, and Brandt had bought the Simpson house on the south end of the island.

The annual Governors' Conference was held at the Sagamore Hotel July 11 to 14, 1954, hosted by Governor Thomas Dewey of New York State and attended by the governors of all 48 states. Although President Dwight D. Eisenhower was slated to address the group, the sudden illness and death of his sister-in-law, Mrs. Milton

Eisenhower, prevented his attendance. In his stead, Vice President Richard M. Nixon delivered the keynote address. One of his themes was the beauty of Lake George and the hospitality of the Sagamore.

In 1958, the Lake George Association filed a pollution complaint against the owners of the Sagamore under the criminal subdivision of section 1153 of the Public Health Law. The charge against the hotel owners was "permitting sewerage to enter Lake George." Cyrus Woodbury of Diamond Point, the executive vice president of the Lake George Association, was very active in pressing the complaint. In a trial held on October 3, 1958, before Justice of the Peace James Ross, the hotel was ordered to pay a fine of $250.

That same year, the Bolton town board approved the establishment of a municipal sewer system. However, in order to make it economically feasible it was imperative that the Sagamore agree to be included in the sewer district. The Sagamore's assessed valuation made up more than 50 percent of the total. Brandt, knowing that he could not continue with his old septic system, was left with little choice. He agreed to have the hotel property included in the district, thus ensuring the success of the project.

In 1962, the Conservation Department purchased a parcel of land from Philip and Aletha Walker. Located on the northwest side of the island, the property included a boathouse and two boat-storage buildings. The state paid $25,000 for this parcel, which was formerly owned by Albert Judson, George Knapp, and Ernest Granger.

Between 1964 and the present, the DEC constructed on this property two boathouses, one marine workshop, and one office complex with storage and workshop areas. It later became the administrative headquarters for all of the lake's state-owned islands—including camping and day-use islands—as well as for the navigational aids on the lake. The marine maintenance center is responsible for the maintenance and repair of all DEC marine equipment, including boats and barges. DEC's Director of Lands and Forests Victor Glider was instrumental in ensuring funding for construction and equipment for the headquarters.

Brandt oversaw the operations of the Sagamore until 1980. By then, it had become difficult for the hotel to attract guests who were without a car, as train service to Lake George and bus service to Bolton had been discontinued. Additionally, in order to bring the hotel into compliance with new fire regulations, Brandt knew that he would have to invest large sums of money. Thus, he decided not to open the hotel for the 1981 season.

In November 1981, Brandt, as president of Sagolf, signed a contract of sale with Philadelphia resident Norman Wolgin, a Lake George summer resident. The negotiations continued over the next year. As supervisor of Bolton at the time, I was involved in several meetings with Brandt and Wolgin. In September 1982, the sale was finalized, with the hotel complex on Green Island and the golf course on the mainland being sold for $5 million.

Wolgin and his architects made a number of changes to the island complex. The main hotel was gutted and insulated. Although the interior was changed dramatically, the exterior design was preserved. The main hotel building is now listed on the National Register of Historic Places.

Wolgin also added a new convention center that can seat 800 for meals, an indoor sports facility, new tennis courts, a large indoor swimming pool, an exercise complex, and three new restaurants. He also commissioned the construction of a 120-passenger cruise ship named *The Morgan*. The ship, built by local boatbuilder William Morgan, has a dining room which can seat 80. The golf course was restored to its original beauty, with underground sprinklers installed. Two lots on the north end of the island were sold, and private, year-round residences were built by William Morgan and Robert Weichbrodt. Wolgin also added 240 rooms with condominium units on the two top floors. There are 60 of these condominiums, each with one or two bedrooms. The owners have use of the newly created docking space on the northeast side of the island, as well as of the hotel's facilities.

In the course of redeveloping the resort, Wolgin formed a new partnership, called Green Island Associates, with Kennington Ltd., Inc., of Los Angeles. The town of Bolton awarded the partnership a $5 million Federal Urban Development Action grant. To date, $1

The Sagamore Hotel on Green Island. © *Richard K. Dean*

million has been repaid, with the remaining $4 million scheduled to be paid as the hotel makes a profit. The venture has shown financial gains each year. The resort, now open year round, was managed by the Omni Hotels Management Company for the first 10 years after its restoration. When the contract expired in July 1995, the Sagamore became independent. Omni Managing Director Robert McIntosh remained with the hotel, which is now affiliated with Preferred Hotels and Resorts Worldwide, an association of independent, four-star, four-diamond properties. The Sagamore, the only four-star resort in New York State, employs 240 staff members year round and 750 during the months of June to September. The expansive sweep of green lawns, shrubbery, and white birches, the friendliness paired with luxury, the atmosphere of peace and relaxation make this hotel exceptional.

With an assessed valuation of $40 million, Green Island is by far the most valuable island on Lake George. The taxes paid by the owners as well as the sales tax revenue have been a real boon to both the town and the county. We all hope that the resort continues to prosper.

LOG BAY ISLAND

THIS STATE-OWNED island, measuring over four acres in size, is located at the entrance to the lovely and peaceful Log Bay. The island's name stems from the vast amount of logging done on the nearby slopes on the lake's eastern shore. The logs were skidded on a daily basis down the mountains and brought to Log Bay where, during the winter months, they were piled on the ice. The lumberjacks chained logs from both ends of the island across to the mainland, thus preventing the logs from floating out of the bay when ice-out occurred. During the months from ice-out until late fall, the loggers continued to store logs in the bay, which served as a kind of corral.

The logs were formed into rafts and pulled across the lake by small, steam-powered boats to sawmills in Bolton. Logs occasionally broke free during heavy windstorms and were scattered around the lake. They floated just under the surface of the lake, often causing serious damage to boats which collided with them. Eventually, the logs became waterlogged and sank. Many of these logs, particularly those of oak, can still be found on the bottom of the lake today.

In 1901, a law was passed forbidding rafting or floating of logs on Lake George between July 1 and October 1. A law passed in 1904 further provided that all rafted logs must be secured and clearly marked to identify the owner.

In later years, after wagon roads were built, many of the logs rafted to Bolton were then transported to sawmills in Caldwell (now the town of Lake George) and Ticonderoga.

The shoreline and the land in the Log Bay area are now owned by the state of New York. This means that, as part of the New York State Forest Preserve, this timberland will never again be harvested.

A camping island until 1960, Log Bay Island has since that time been used as a cruiser-camping island, with dockage for 12 boats. The island is ideal for that purpose, as the cruisers float peacefully in the calm and tranquil waters of the bay adjacent to the island.

Many years ago, the southeast end of this island was struck by lightning. Two campers, asleep in their tent, were knocked off their cots by the lightning. Fortunately, they did not require any medical attention but, in their own words, it was an experience they would never forget.

I remember that in the 1940s the cove at the isthmus of Log Bay Island was covered with lovely white water lilies. Today, however, these lilies are no longer present.

Just east of Log Bay Island is Shelving Rock Bay, the shoreline of which is also owned by the state. The shallow water and sandy bottom of this bay make it a popular place for boaters to toss out their anchor. Youngsters especially enjoy the excellent swimming here. However, the increasing number of boats anchoring here is beginning to create problems. The water clarity is decreasing and activity on the shoreline is definitely a cause for concern.

Hopefully, the Lake George Park Commission will address this problem in the near future, as it has in Paradise Bay, so that future generations will be able to enjoy an environmentally sound Log Bay and Shelving Rock Bay.

HEN & CHICKENS ISLANDS

OW THIS group of five islands derived its name is not clear.
Perhaps chickens were once raised here. A more likely
explanation, however, is that some clever soul viewed the largest island
as a mother hen, with the four smaller ones being her baby chicks.
Anyone flying over the Hen & Chickens group today cannot fail to
notice that the "mother hen" exhibits a remarkable similarity to a
chicken perched on a roost. Most assuredly, however, whoever
originally gave the group its name—sometime during the nineteenth
century—did so without ever having had a bird's eye view of them.

The first recorded history of the mother hen island, as I shall call
the large one, begins in 1889, when Captain Delavan Bloodgood, a
surgeon in the U. S. Navy, built a bungalow on the west side of the
island. The house faced Green Island, where the Sagamore Hotel had
recently opened its doors. Bloodgood's cottage was unique, constructed
in the fashion of an East Indian bungalow. It remained on the island for
several years even after passage of the state law providing for the
removal of all structures from state-owned islands. Eventually,
however, it was moved across the ice to Watch Point, a privately owned
piece of land on the east shore, about a mile and a half south of Hen &
Chickens. Purchased by the Robinson family, the bungalow was later
enlarged and today still is used by the Robinsons as a summer
residence.

The islands in the Hen & Chickens group have had more than
their share of unfortunate incidents. Campsite 1, for instance, had an
abundance of poison ivy which I and the other rangers tried to
eradicate over the years. Back in the 1960s, we did it with 2-4 D,
taking care only to spray the poison ivy plants, since this herbicide

Hen & Chickens Islands, looking north into the Narrows.   © *Richard K. Dean*

also kills other vegetation. Today, the DEC wisely prohibits the use of all herbicides and pesticides on state-owned islands.

I remember one particular group of campers who, confronted with this annoying plant on their campsite, decided to take matters into their own hands. Without bothering to don gardening gloves, they set about pulling the weeds by hand. It was not long thereafter that Dr. Leonard Busman, a Bolton physician, had a visit from these amateur gardeners who were, shall we say, not exactly happy campers.

The Hen & Chickens islands seem to be prone to disaster. On August 14, 1981, John D. Murray of Caldwell, New Jersey, on his way to visit friends near Tongue Mountain, crashed his seaplane into one of the islands at about 9:30 in the evening. Ranger Richard Kober recounted after the accident, "There was a family [camping] on the island and they tried to wave flashlights at the pilot. The people said that if he had continued straight, he would have run into their picnic table." Murray swerved at the last minute, and one wing hit the water while the other hit a tree on one of the islands. Hearing the crash, Sherwood Finley, who lived on nearby Fourteen Mile Island, rushed to the scene. The Bolton Rescue Squad and Sergeant Fenton Sabo of the Lake George Park Commission were quick to respond. Although Murray's passenger, Mary Jensen, suffered a broken elbow, and the plan, was completely destroyed, it was fortunate that there were no serious injuries.

A far more tragic accident, a freak of nature, occurred on June 5, 1979. A storm warning had been issued that morning and DEC park ranger Rich Kober checked the islands to advise campers that high winds might be on their way. Three Bolton Landing teenagers— Victoria Dodge, Joan Baldwin, and Sherrie Snyder—were enjoying an overnight camping trip on one of the Hen & Chickens Islands when Kober pulled up in his boat. Heeding the ranger's advice, the girls made sure that their boat was securely tied to the dock; they carried their canoe up onto the island.

When the storm did hit, it brought driving rains and hurricane-strength winds, forcing the girls to take shelter. The wind was so strong that it picked up their canoe, rolling it toward the lake. As they rushed to save it, the girls ran past one of the island's giant white pines. Just at that moment, the tree was suddenly uprooted and sent crashing to the ground. It all happened so quickly that one of the three, Victoria Dodge, had no chance to get out of the way. She was struck by the tree. Repeated attempts by Vickie's friends to revive her were futile. As Warren County Coroner Dr. Leonard Busman would later confirm, she was killed instantly. Frantic, the two girls sought shelter by lying down behind the fireplace of one of the campsites and waited for the storm to let up. When it finally did, they rushed by boat over to Fourteen Mile Island to call the Glen Island Ranger Station. From there, Ranger Curt Truax immediately called me at DEC headquarters on Green Island, as well as notifying the Bolton Rescue Squad. We all responded immediately but, of course, it was too late.

The sad task of notifying Vickie's parents fell to me. The accident left Boltonians in a state of shock and sorrow. Vickie had been a popular student, an outstanding athlete, head drum majorette of the school band, a cheerleader, and junior prom queen. Her death was a tragic loss not only for her family and friends but also for the entire community.

FOURTEEN MILE ISLAND

FOURTEEN MILE Island, which is privately owned, is located on the east side of the lake, near Shelving Rock Mountain. It is not clear where the name Fourteen Mile comes from since the island actually is only 11 miles from the southern end of the lake. In the past, it has also been called Kenesaw and Beardsley's.

A narrow channel, affectionately referred to by some as Lover's Lane, separates this picturesque island from the mainland. Boats passing through this channel must reduce their speed to five miles per hour.

On March 6, 1857, the state of New York sold this island to William Smith of Albany. At the same time, Smith also purchased Dome, Clay, Crown, Oahu, and Turtle Islands, paying a total of $400 for the six islands. He built a small hunting lodge on Fourteen Mile Island, leasing it to George Durrin, who operated the lodge under the name of Durrin's Hotel. The hotel was located on the island's west shore near the old steamboat dock. The cribbing of this dock can still be seen today in the water. John Whalen of Glens Falls is the current owner of the lot.

Smith's will, recorded in 1869, stated that the island had been leased to Durrin rent free. It also indicated that Durrin was to be the caretaker for all six islands and that he could renew his lease.

Upon his death, Smith willed an island to each of his five surviving children, with the sixth island going to his granddaughter, the child of Smith's deceased daughter. It was Smith's wish that the islands remain in possession of the family. Erastus Smith, son of William, inherited Fourteen Mile Island, subsequently gaining possession of several of the other islands.

Not wishing to operate the hotel himself, Erastus hired R. G. Bradley and Company to manage it. The hotel, later enlarged and renamed Fourteen Mile Island House, became the setting for a myriad of social events in an attempt to attract more guests.

Guests spent many a merry evening at the hotel, dancing and enjoying the music. Erastus, a ladies' man who remained a bachelor throughout his life, frequently was seen at these events.

In 1875, Reuben Bradley left the Fourteen Mile Island establishment to build a hotel of his own on the mainland at the foot of Shelving Rock. This nearby competition, which was named the Hundred Island House, was apparently the impetus which made Erastus Smith decide to sell Fourteen Mile and Oahu Islands, retaining only Turtle Island.

Lawn and dock, Fourteen Mile Island.

Courtesy Crandall Public Library's Center for Folklife, History and Cultural Programs (Glens Falls, NY)

In 1884, General Peter Bellinger of Elizabeth, New Jersey, bought the island for $10,000 in a court-ordered auction for back taxes. The next year, General Bellinger purchased Oahu Island.

In 1888, the Lake George Steamboat Company decided that the island would be an ideal location for passengers on the cruise ships to go ashore for picnics, a swim, and relaxation. General Bellinger, however, was unwilling to sell the island for these purposes. In a clever ploy, the Steamboat Company decided to have Thomas Wicker act as its agent in purchasing the property.

Wicker appeared at the island hotel and became very friendly with Bellinger. When Wicker offered $10,000 for the island, Bellinger accepted, not realizing that Wicker was a front man for the Steamboat Company. Wicker collected a tidy commission of $5,000 for his efforts, and Bellinger was one angry man indeed when he discovered that Wicker had pulled the wool over his eyes.

On the night of August 3, 1893, one of the small steamers, the *Rachel*, was involved in a tragic accident while transporting passengers from the Fourteen Mile Island House to the Hundred Island House.

It seems that Claude Granger, an employee of the Fourteen Mile Island House, took over the job of piloting the *Rachel* when the regular captain became ill. In the darkness, the steamer crashed into a submerged pier and sank in about 10 feet of water in a matter of minutes. Guests from the Hundred Island House rushed to the scene with rowboats, trying to rescue the 23 passengers. However, nine passengers, including a mother and son, lost their lives that night. Some of the victims were not found until the next morning. The bodies were recovered and found temporary resting places on the billiard tables of the hotel.

It is said that this tragedy claimed more lives than any other single boating accident on Lake George. In my research, I have not found any evidence to the contrary.

By 1896, the excursions to the island had become less popular and less profitable, and the Steamboat Company decided to close the hotel. In 1905 the island was sold to William H. Beardsley for use as a summer residence. Beardsley was a railroad executive with New York

Central Railroad and the Florida Central Railroad. Beardsley died in December 1925. When his wife Lillian passed away in 1931, ownership of the island passed to their son and daughter, Sterling S. Beardsley and Lillian B. Gledhill. In 1941, Lillian sold her share to Sterling, who died in the late 1940s. Sterling's grandchildren, Henry Beardsley and Betty B. King, then inherited the island.

I still remember their speedboat *Betty*, which used to cruise through the islands and back and forth to Bolton. Ralph Stiles Sr., from West Fort Ann, was the island caretaker for many years. His son, Ralph Stiles Jr., was the caretaker for the Knapp Estate on the east shore for many years.

I was stationed at the Glen Island ranger's headquarters in 1953 when a fire broke out in the ice house on Fourteen Mile Island. It was just after midnight, and the flames could be seen for many miles. I rushed to the island, as did the Bolton Fire Department. Upon our arrival, the fire was blazing out of control, but the firefighters were able to confine it, preventing damage to other buildings on the island.

Over the years, the Beardsleys found that they were using the island less and less. In 1959, they decided to subdivide it and sell it. Several lots were sold to owners who subsequently built homes on the island. One of them was Richard Bartlett, a former state legislator, judge, and dean of the Albany Law School. Remson Kinne, long-time island camper, and John Whalen of Glens Falls also bought lots.

Kinne's property is now owned by Herman Bergman of Philadelphia. James Lafferty, a General Electric engineer from Schenectady, purchased a lot with an on-land boathouse on the north end of the island, converting the boathouse into a cozy residence. (In the late-nineteenth century, boat owners often built these on-land boathouses in which to store their boats during the winter months. They were built close enough to the water so that the boats could be launched using hand winches and railway tracks.)

Doctor John DeLong, now deceased, purchased a large home on the east side of the island, later selling it to Harold Tucker and Marvin Eger of Bayonne, New Jersey. Tucker was postmaster of Bayonne, and Eger, now deceased, was the city's comptroller. The Tucker-Eger property was later divided, and is now owned by the sons, Lawrence Tucker of Dayton, Ohio and Richard and Jeffrey Eger of Morristown, New Jersey.

In 1961, Sherwood Finley, an artist now residing on Sanibel Island, Florida, purchased the large house on the southwest end of the island, as well as the boathouse with a second floor apartment, from Henry Beardsley and Betty King. I am indebted to Sherwood Finley and his brother Gardner who provided me with a wealth of information about the island and its history.

Like so many of the Lake George islands, Fourteen Mile Island was not spared from bloodshed during the Revolutionary War era. It is reported that a party led by Major Wait Hopkins and including 14 officers, two women and a nine-year-old boy left Fort George on July 15, 1779, to gather huckleberries on Fourteen Mile Island. While on the island, they were surprised by a scouting party consisting of 24 Indians and three white men who killed nine members of Hopkins's group and captured the remainder. Although the dead men were scalped and two prisoners were wounded, it is reported that neither the women nor the child were harmed.

I close this chapter on Fourteen Mile Island with the hope that the future occupants will continue to enjoy this lovely island and treat it with as much care as the present owners have done.

85

OAHU ISLAND

OAHU ISLAND, located near the point of Tongue Mountain, is one of 30 islands which was sold by the government prior to the passage of the 1876 law forbidding the state from selling any Lake George islands. Throughout its history, it has borne several names, including Floa, Flea, Flora, and Bellinger Island.

As early as the 1880s, Seneca Ray Stoddard noted that General P. T. Bellinger of Elizabeth, New Jersey, owned the island, living in a cottage on the southern part. J. W. Moore, chief engineer, U. S. Navy, occupied the cottage near the northern end of the island.

General Bellinger had two daughters and one son who inherited Bellinger's Island from the general, retaining ownership until 1952. It is said that the daughters, Georgia and Elizabeth, did not hold their brother Gus in great esteem and, in fact, refused to have anything to do with him. Georgia and Elizabeth, neither of whom ever married, resided on the island, traveling back and forth to the mainland by rowboat. Despite the fact that Oahu lies in a part of the lake considered by boaters to be one of the roughest, these remarkable and extremely independent ladies were never deterred by high waters. On the contrary, they were highly insulted whenever someone in a powerboat offered to help them. They were quick, however, to help others in trouble. I remember an incident when a boating party, surprised by sudden high winds, took refuge at the Bellingers' dock. The sisters rowed to Pearl Point, where they used the Knapp family's telephone to call for a taxi boat to come and rescue the stranded boaters.

Georgia and Elizabeth returned to the island every year until both were well into their eighties. Every summer, they would load their rowboat with provisions, bedrolls, and a lantern, and row the entire length of the lake, camping on islands or points along the mainland when night fell. Throughout the summer, they rowed their boat to the mainland each Sunday to attend church services regardless of the weather. They could be recognized from afar by their old-fashioned poke bonnets, tied with a bow at the chin, which they always wore while out in their boat.

Old-timers who knew these grand old ladies like to relate the story of how "the Bellingers did not prefer bathing suits when swimming." In fact, rumor had it that the two ladies were frequently observed while skinny-dipping and that a neighbor living a half mile away used a telescope to observe them bathing.

The state of New York was interested in purchasing the island from the Bellingers and turning it into a camping or day-use area. Located at the southern entrance to the Narrows, this island was the last of the privately owned ones from here to a point six miles to the north. William Foss, Director of Lands and Forest in the New York State Conservation Department, attempted to negotiate a sale with the Bellingers which would have included a provision granting the sisters a lifetime lease on the island.

I personally attempted to develop a friendship with these ladies, hoping I could convince them to sell the island to the state. What I discovered, in talking with the sisters, was that they did not want any intruders on their island. They told me of their concern that inconsiderate campers and fishermen would build fires and leave litter on their island. As I talked to them more and more, my belief grew ever firmer that there was no way that the state would ever own Bellingers Island.

In the 1940s, Elizabeth Bellinger passed away, leaving Georgia as the sole owner of the island. Georgia decided in 1952 to sell the island. But she was firm in her commitment to sell only to someone who would care for and preserve the island as the Bellingers had done during the decades they had owned it. She found her buyer in Lawrence Ferguson of Kew Gardens, New York., who offered her $18,000 for the property. Ignoring the standing offer of $25,000 from the state, Georgia Bellinger accepted Ferguson's bid.

The new owner divided the island, selling half of it to his brother Irving Ferguson. Lawrence and Irving, each of whom had two children, gave the island property to them in the early 1970s. The island has four houses, two of which are still owned by the Ferguson children. Of the other two, one was sold in 1988 to Dr. Patricia A. Fox of Schenectady, while the other was purchased in 1995 by the Gerald Malovany family of northern Virginia.

SHIP ISLAND

SHIP ISLAND, a state-owned island located just northeast of Oahu Island, is the most southerly island of the Narrows. Ship owes its name to the fact that its trees once resembled a ship, with a large tree in the center as the mast. However, ice push, wind and waves created both by the wake of power boats and by the wind, have devastated this island in recent years.

When R. E. Doherty surveyed Ship Island on August 7, 1917, he recorded the existence of pine, cedar, white birch, maple, and numerous tag alders on the island. On May 12, 1995, Chester Sims, Shirley Dean, and I inspected Ship Island and counted 12 white cedars, three large maples (one with seven trunks), two large paper birches, several small white pines, and numerous tag alder.

The 80-foot white pine which served as the mast fell into the lake in 1992, uprooting a large mass of soil. Destructive wave action subsequently attacked this narrow part of the island. If something is not done to protect the island, the lake will soon sever it into two parts. It is sad for me to see the deterioration of this island's former beauty.

Chester, Shirley, and I decided to try to restore the island to its condition of 30 to 40 years ago and prevent further erosion. This would require rip-rapping the entire perimeter of the island, along with fill consisting of gravel and top soil. Planting of more small white pines and a ground cover of crown vetch would also be beneficial in restoring this island to its former condition. We worked out a detailed proposal of how this could be accomplished, and DEC personnel have assured us that they will cooperate and assist us in our endeavor if funding becomes available. Sadly, Chester passed away on March 13, 1996, before he could see the project brought to fruition.

89

Ship Island, along with many other islands suffering from soil erosion, also was a concern close to the heart of John Apperson. Apperson (1879–1964) was one of the earliest environmental activists on Lake George. Apperson's activities on Lake George are detailed in a separate chapter of this book.

Batteries housed on Ship Island are used to generate power for a navigation light located just a few feet east of the island. This light, which is visible from the east side of Long Island, some six miles to the south, was placed there for the safety and convenience of boaters trying to navigate the Narrows after dark. If boaters guide their vessels toward this light, the beam will lead them to the entrance of the Narrows from where they can proceed to the main channel.

Ship Island, because of its small size, is not suitable for camping. However, over the years, we found several people using it for that purpose. These people were generally canoeists with pup tents. As a rule, we never let them stay overnight. But if they had arrived by canoe and had been forced onto this island by rough waters, we also did not make them leave in the middle of the night.

I remember a spot off the southeast end of Ship Island, in about 30 feet of water, which was at one time an excellent place to fish for smallmouth bass. Any bass fishermen reading this chapter might want to try their luck there again.

Ship Island.   *Photo by Dick Swire*

Turtle Island

TURTLE ISLAND, now a state island with 33 campsites and over a
mile of shoreline, was originally sold by the state for $25 to Almon
N. Wakefield in November 1861. Wakefield later sold the island to
William Smith of Albany.

When Smith's son Erastus inherited Turtle Island, he decided to
build a cottage on it. Known as Green Oaks, the home was located on
a level area on the east side of the island, at today's campsite 24.
Although the island's terrain made it difficult to locate a building site,
Erastus managed to find an ideal spot.

In the latter part of the nineteenth century, Old Rastus, as he was
called by the locals, lived on the island with no means of
transportation. He would hitch a ride into town or to another island
by flagging down passing boats. His sister Julia also periodically
occupied the island. In the 1890s, Smith unsuccessfully attempted to
sell Turtle Island by distributing a flyer announcing the sale. It was
not until 1923 that he finally sold the island. The buyer was the state
of New York, which paid $14,000.

This island is located just off the shore of Point of Tongue
Mountain, on the west side of the lake. The name Turtle may derive
from the fact that the island's shores are an ideal spot for turtles to lay
their eggs, though we never had any reports during my tenure of
campers finding turtle eggs. Actually, the area best known for turtle
breeding is Log Bay. The island's name most assuredly does not come
from its shape, which, far from resembling a turtle, is more
reminiscent of a poodle. Seen from above, the island's vegetation
appears remarkably similar to a poodle's curly coat.

On Labor Day weekend of 1957, tragedy struck when two Boy

Scouts from Brooklyn drowned in the waters off this island. The boys, who were camping with their troop on Turtle, were out in a 16-foot aluminum boat with their scout master and another scout when the boat filled with water and capsized about 20 feet north of Turtle Island. The scout master was able to bring one of the boys to safety, but the other two were trapped under the boat. Campers from nearby Mohican Island, hearing the cries for help, dashed into the water to assist. But all help came too late.

For more than an hour, Dr. Leonard Busman of Bolton Landing and I attempted to resuscitate the boys. We all were deeply saddened by the loss of life of these two young boys.

The island's proximity to the Tongue Mountain shore makes Turtle an ideal place for raccoons to scavenge for food. Many campers over the years have been the victims of the raccoons' voracious appetites. Experienced campers have learned to take precautions to prevent the pilfering of their breakfast, lunch, and dinner makings. In former times they would keep their food supplies in a sturdy bag hung from a limb of a tree at least four feet above ground level. With today's securely latched coolers, it is enough to keep edibles locked away in these. In any case, campers should be cautioned never to keep food inside of their tents. Bacon seems to be a favorite treat—not only for campers but also for the raccoons. We often used live traps containing bacon or bacon grease as bait in our attempts to capture these pesky critters.

Another annoying creature occasionally found on Turtle Island is the long-bodied timber rattlesnake, which gets its name from its wooded habitat. These snakes can easily swim across the narrow channel between the island and Tongue Mountain. During my 42 years of service on the lake, I believe that I or my colleagues killed at least two dozen snakes on Turtle Island. Until a 1971 state law outlawed payment of bounties, Warren County paid a $5 bounty to anyone presenting 2 or 3 inches of the tail, with the rattles intact, to the town clerk. In 1983, the state added the rattlesnake to its list of endangered species, making it illegal to kill them.

It is important to point out that no island camper has ever been bitten by a rattlesnake. And, although a few people have been bitten on the mainland, there is no record of any deaths in this area resulting from a rattlesnake bite.

Around 1970, a large bear swam over to Turtle and ran the entire length of the island. Although the campers were startled, none was harmed. Following his dash across the island, the bear leaped into the water and swam to the lake's east shore, climbing out near Pearl Point. I was fortunate to witness the bear from my boat as he swam the last 200 feet to the mainland. Although several campers took photos of the incident, I did not have my camera on board so I have no picture to add to my collection of Lake George oddities. Perhaps someone reading this chapter still has a photo of that unusual incident.

MOHICAN ISLAND

THIS STATE-OWNED island is located in the Narrows group, just east of Turtle Island. The name undoubtedly comes from James Fenimore Cooper's novel, *The Last of the Mohicans*, which is set in the area around Lake George. In 1917 a sign on the island declared its name as Phelps Island. Various state maps dated 1919 record it as Phelps, Mohican, and Pleasure Island. The 1923 state recreational circular with map designated it as Mohican Island.

In the late 1800s summer homes were built on the northern end and on the southwestern end of the island. However, when the state began enforcing its 1885 law prohibiting permanent structures on the islands, these summer camps were removed. The remains of dock cribbing, submerged stone piers, and steps are still evident today.

Another unique characteristic of the island is the presence of two pot holes, also called Indian kettles, on the western shore.

This island, with its nine campsites, is ideal for camping. It is wooded, though some of the campsites are quite sunny. Campsites 2, 4, and 9 are popular for their shallow-water swimming areas, while sites 1, 3, and 5 have spacious areas for tents.

In 1992, Mohican Island was at the center of a controversy over DEC policy allowing the removal of dead and hazardous trees on state-owned camping islands on Lake George. Although the policy actually was instituted a few years prior to 1992, the tree-cutting project on Mohican was what really brought it to the public's attention.

For many years before I began working for the state in 1941, and up until 1986, dead and dangerous trees were removed from the islands as soon as possible after being reported. At no time was an excessive number of trees cut down. Campers were fined for cutting down any healthy or diseased trees at all.

However, the Mohican Island incident indicated a new direction in policy. Dr. Robert Rosen, who had been camping on Mohican Island for 40 years, first brought the problem to the attention of the town of Bolton in June of 1992. The town sent its zoning administrator, Joseph Deppe, assisted by Edward Ross and Dick Swire, to Mohican to survey the damage. Their survey reported that 82 trees had been cut, 21 of which were live trees with no sign of disease. The trees ranged in size from less than 21 inches in diameter to over 40 inches. The group took photographs of many of the trees as well as of large piles of limbs, leaves, and brush.

Dr. Rosen, the Bolton Town Board, the Lake George Association and I led a crusade to protest this new tree-cutting policy. Many letters were written to and received from the DEC. The DEC justified its policy of removing dead and hazardous trees as necessary to protect campers from injuries.

In my opinion, a healthy tree in shallow soil poses a greater danger to the camping public than a diseased tree growing in deep soil. A dead tree is less likely to be toppled by wind because of its lack of foliage. If a dead tree does fall, it poses less of a hazard to campers than a live tree because it is less dense.

In the autumn of 1992, DEC removed trees on Uncas, Sunny, and Little Harbor Islands, cutting a total of 119 dead and dangerous trees, though this time in a prudent manner. Wood chippers were used to dispose of the brush, and the chips were used for mulching, which actually improved the areas. It seems that, fortunately, the injudicious cutting was limited to Mohican Island.

During the past few years, the DEC has curtailed its program, removing only those trees which actually threaten the safety of campers. Budget restraints have undoubtedly played a role in curbing the extent of tree removal. Whatever the reason for halting the program, most of us hope that never again will another incident of this nature occur on any island on Lake George.

Ranger Island

RANGER ISLAND is a state-owned island in the Narrows, west of Pearl Point. A pretty cottage with a sharply peaked tower once was located on the northern end of the island. The house, built sometime prior to 1889, belonged to Justice Frederick E. Ranger of Glens Falls. It was from this family that the island derived its name.

The cottage was removed when the state claimed ownership of the island under the provision of the 1876 law which prohibited the sale of any state islands on Lake George. The 30 islands which had already been sold prior to passage were exempt.

Ranger Island, with its two campsites, is ideal for families with small children. A small sandy cove at the northeastern end of the island makes a wonderful spot for tots to wade and play in the water. The wooded island provides good shade, and the surrounding waters are rich in smallmouth bass.

I remember Isadore (Izzy) Swire, a long-time camper and excellent fisherman, who caught his bass limit many times off Ranger Island. The Swire family camped in the Narrows for almost 50 years. Izzy was not only a true gentleman but also an expert in electrical engineering. He volunteered his services many times to help us repair the generator on Glen Island. Izzy gave up camping on Ranger Island when the Swire family purchased Three Brother Islands in 1950. Until his death in the 1970s, he continued to use his carpentry, plumbing, and electrical skills to keep all the homes on that island in a good state of repair.

When Izzy moved from Ranger to his new home, he left some of his camping equipment at the campsite for other campers to use. Dick Swire, who today lives on Three Brother Islands year round, recently related the following story to me about Izzy's old campsite.

It seems that Arthur and Audrey Goldberg of New Jersey first came to Lake George on a camping vacation in the early 1950s. Not knowing what to expect, they brought along everything they thought they might need for an adventure in the Adirondack wilderness. Upon arriving at Glen Island headquarters, they were assigned campsite 1 on Ranger Island, the site that Izzy Swire had camped on for so many years. Much to the Goldbergs' surprise, they discovered when they docked at the island that the site was well equipped for campers. It had not only a water pump, but also a kerosene refrigerator. Camping wasn't such a primitive adventure after all, they thought to themselves.

They decided to return the next summer, this time without all the "excess" baggage of coolers and water containers. After all, they thought, they wouldn't need these on the Lake George islands. However, this time they were assigned to a different island, and their campsite looked so different from that of the previous year. When they went to Glen Island to ask why the water pump and refrigerator were missing from their site, the ranger smiled and explained that Ranger 1's comforts were definitely the exception, not the rule.

Ranger Island has always been one of my favorites, and surely the favorite of the many youngsters who have splashed in the waters and played in the sand at its small beach over the years.

UNCAS ISLAND

U NCAS IS a state-owned island consisting of 14 campsites on six acres. It is located just west of Glen and Phantom Islands and south of Big Burnt. The island was named for Chief Uncas, the hero in James Fenimore Cooper's classic novel, *The Last of the Mohicans*, in which Lake George played an important role.

In 1883, L. H. Fillmore of Ticonderoga established a photo studio on Uncas, specializing in scenes of Lake George. He also constructed a crude but functional darkroom which he made available to other amateur photographers. In addition to his photo-finishing services, he also supplied local advertisers with photographs. His rates for photo finishing were reasonable; in fact, he charged nothing at all if the photographs were of Lake George.

Uncas Island is nicely wooded, with an abundance of rock ledges and large masses of stone on the west side where several elevated campsites are found. These rocky campsites have always been particularly popular with campers who, in years past, actually assigned them names. Campsite 10, for example, was referred to as The Rock while campsite 15 was called Goat Hill and campsite 14 bore the name Alcatraz. Other campsites were referred to as The Point (8), The Hole (6) and Broadway and 42nd Street (1). In the late 1880s, site 1 had a cottage on it.

These names were in common usage during the era when campers could camp for most of the summer on one particular site. Present-day campers are probably not aware of the names, unless, of course, they are the children or grandchildren of these former campers. I remember well many of these families. Long-lasting friendships grew up among these campers, their children, and grandchildren. They held cookouts together and staged song fests; their children played hide-and-seek and island tag together. I remember fondly the square dances held at campsite 3 with music furnished by the campers. In my mind, these were the good old days, even if we sometimes had to enforce the "quiet and order" rules and regulations ordering quiet between the hours of 10 PM and 7 AM. Many of these former campers now own homes in Bolton or Hague.

I can also recall some incidents on Uncas which were humorous, as well as a few which were hazardous. Any prank, misbehavior, or mischief could generally be attributed to "Dennis the Menace" who, as a youngster, caused his family and other campers much consternation over the years. I remember searching the island for several hours one evening looking for Dennis, who had disappeared. We finally found him sound asleep in an extra tent on a campsite on the opposite side of the island. Dennis was basically a good boy; he simply had an extra helping of mischief in him. Today, Dennis is a General Electric foreman in Schenectady and still visits his family's home in Hague.

Of course, Dennis had friends on the island who also did not always behave like little gentlemen. I remember the time when one of these friends, Steve, got into a quarrel with his brother George, resulting in Steve hitting George over the head with a hammer. Their father Max raced to Glen Island to report the injury which, though serious, did not require the services of a doctor. We were able to patch George up with our first aid kit. George has not returned to Lake George in recent years. But Steve, now a college professor, owns a cottage in Northwest Bay, where he vacations each year. He swears to this day that he never intended to harm his brother.

Then there was Laurie, who was a quiet loner amidst the boisterous young campers on Uncas. Laurie got his kicks on the island by running to his dock and jumping into the family's rowboat every time a fast boat sped by his campsite. He loved the faster boats and enjoyed the rocking action caused by the motor boat swell. His mother, however, was not a fan of the motorboats and came to Glen Island to complain about the dangers they posed to other boaters and canoeists.

I remember another family who camped on Uncas Island in the late 1940s and early 1950s. The family had a son, David, who liked to row his boat over to Glen Island every day to chat with me. The family's name was Geffen and today David is one of Hollywood's top producers. He is the co-founder, with Steven Spielberg and Jeffrey Katzenberg, of DreamWorks Studio, and the former owner of Geffen Records. In July 1996, David wrote me a letter in which he reminisced about his childhood camping experiences on Uncas Island. I'd like to share part of his letter with you:

> As I recall, my expeditions across the lake to spend time with you were an important part of my summer vacation, and a responsibility that I took quite seriously. I can only imagine what entertaining tales I must have had to share with you!
>
> If there's one thing that stands out in my mind about our yearly camping trips to Lake George, it's probably that my family felt like more of a unit there than in any other setting. At home in Brooklyn, it seemed like we rarely sat down together in the same room; my mother worked tirelessly at running her shop, my father's job kept him very busy as well, and my brother and I behaved like typical kids, running in different directions.
>
> Once we arrived on Uncas Island, however, and had pitched our tents and marked our territory and settled in, we had the chance to hang out together like a traditional family, and get to know each other—for better or for worse! I'll always remember those camping trips as happy, wonderfully relaxing times.

GLEN ISLAND

GLEN ISLAND, a state-owned island, serves as the Department of Environmental Conservation's main headquarters on Lake George for the issuance of camping and day-use permits. It is located in the Narrows, about three miles north of Bolton Landing.

Glen Island has the distinction of being the only island on Lake George ever to have been the site of a U. S. Post Office (1927 to 1976). It is also the only island on the lake with a commissary.

In 1885, Glen Island, along with 153 other islands on Lake George, were made part of the state Forest Preserve by an act of the legislature. Prior to the passage of this law, Glen Island was occupied by the Glen Club, also known as the Cold Water Club. Its members included many prominent citizens of Glens Falls, among them B. F. and Mortimer Lapham. It was the Lapham family who constructed the quaint stone lighthouse located at the northeast end of Glen Island. Presumably, the name of the island derives from the Glen Club.

Due to the popularity of island camping, the state recognized that it would have to establish some form of permit system and an administrative office for the state islands. Thus, in 1921, it was decided that an island headquarters should be set up, and Glen Island was chosen as the base.

Glen proved to be an ideal location for a ranger station. It was centrally located and readily identifiable by anyone approaching the Narrows. The north end of Glen Island also afforded excellent dockage, sheltered from northerly winds by nearby Phantom Island, and from westerly winds by Uncas Island.

The first ranger to issue camping permits to island campers was

Smith Hastings of Bolton Landing, who served in this position from 1916 to 1920. However, Hastings was not stationed on Glen Island. Instead, he issued the permits from his home on the mainland.

The first ranger to reside on Glen Island was Jay Taylor, who was appointed in 1921. He lived in the cottage which had been built by the Cold Water Club during its tenure on the island. This structure was demolished during the 1930s. Jay was not only an excellent ranger but also a skilled fisherman. Old-timers used to praise him for being able to catch fish in spots where other fishermen could not even get a bite, swearing that he could catch fish out of a bathtub. It is said that Jay ruled the island with an iron hand and that his word was law. When he died in 1936, his wife Amelia was appointed as his replacement. She was well acquainted with the duties, having worked closely with her husband, and performed the job capably and efficiently until her retirement in 1954.

Jay and Amelia Taylor, along with their daughters Helen and Louise, spent one entire winter living on a houseboat anchored in a bay near Uncas Island campsite 1. Helen assisted her mother in the permit office. She married Sam Snyder, and Louise married Robert Boswich.

I began my employment with the New York State Conservation Department in 1941 as a laborer, later working as a campsite caretaker. In 1944 I became a forest ranger, and in 1954 I was appointed as officer in charge of all state-owned islands on the lake. From 1963 to 1973 I served as general park foreman, before being appointed supervisor of Lake George operations, a position which I held until my retirement in 1983.

As island campers increased in numbers, many of them staying on their campsites for the entire summer, the government saw the need for a Post Office on Glen Island. It was established on June 10, 1924. That same year, a public telephone was installed on the island. Mrs. Taylor was appointed postmaster, a position which she held until 1954. The mail was transported daily by boat to and from the Bolton Landing Post Office. This contract was held for many years by the Lamb brothers and Kevin Conerty, with Edward Lamb, Sylvester

Glen Island Headquarters docking area.   © *Richard K. Dean*

Armstrong, Dick Fahey, and Tom Conerty piloting the mail boat. Tom Conerty has piloted many of the large passenger ships on Lake George, including the *Mohican* and the *Ticonderoga*, and is now the captain of the *Lac du Saint Sacrement*, the largest ship on the lake.

In 1953, the government changed the status of the Glen Island Post Office, demoting it to a U. S. Postal Rural Station. My wife Betty was appointed clerk in charge. On August 30, 1975, the U. S. Postal Service eliminated operations on Glen Island completely. The room formerly used as the post office was converted to additional living space and DEC storage space.

In about 1930, the Conservation Department authorized the establishment of a commissary on Glen Island for the sale of food, camping supplies, and dairy products. The commissary was a great boon for the campers, particularly for those who relied on rowboats

103

and canoes for transportation to and from the mainland. Over the years, the commissary has been operated by a number of individuals: Alex (son of Jay) Taylor, Mae Webb, Bernard Buckley, Kevin Conerty, Thomas Conerty and his wife Kathy, and, as of this writing, David Waters.

From 1938 to 1940, the Civilian Conservation Corps had a camp (Camp S-82, Company 204) on the west side of Route 9N, about seven miles north of Bolton Landing. One of the jobs of those of us working in the camp was to remove the existing buildings on Glen Island, consisting of a commissary, post office, living quarters, and an ice house.

The CCC boys (Larry Sheehan of Glens Falls, Bernard Ramsey of Lake George, and Milton Brickner of Bolton Landing were in charge of supervising this troop) erected new buildings in rustic, log-cabin style. These were equipped with electricity and also had indoor plumbing, with water pumped in from the lake. The fact that these buildings still exist today is testimony to the fine craftsmanship of the Civilian Conservation Corps. Except for one structure—that adjacent to the commissary—all of the buildings seen on the island today were built by the CCC.

I did not actually work on the construction, but served instead as mess sergeant. My job was to provide the noon meal for the construction crew. However, I occasionally had the opportunity to visit the island myself and to observe the progress of the construction. Luck was on my side, and in April 1941 I had the extreme good fortune to be hired by the Conservation Department for a job on Glen Island.

The first year, my wife Betty and my daughter Gail—one year old at the time—lived in a 12- by 14-foot tent, which was on a platform, walled up three feet on each side. We stayed in the tent until October, spending many of our evenings fishing for bullheads. Although the buildings on the island contained two apartments, these were occupied by the Taylors and by Walter Harris, a state laborer. When Walt left his job on Glen Island the next year, my family and I were able to move out of the tent and into more permanent quarters. A few years later we were blessed with the birth of our second daughter, Janie. Both of my daughters (Gail Street and Janie Weller) have many fond memories of growing up on Glen Island.

We had many great rangers over the years at Glen Island—among the rangers who worked on Glen Island were Stanley Weller, Bob Rostetter, Curt Truax, Tim Hendricks, Herb Scott, Don O'Brien, and Jim McEananey, Sr. All were very dedicated and greatly admired by all the campers and day users with whom they came in contact.

There are no statistics on the number of individuals who have visited Glen Island since it was first established as camping headquarters. The visitors include campers, sightseers, post office patrons, commissary customers, fishermen, and tour-boat passengers. However, I think it would be safe to say that more people have set foot on this island than any other state island on Lake George. I would estimate that at least a million people have been on this small island over the course of this century.

While some people might think that living on an island less than .75 acre in size would be very dull, my years on Glen Island proved to be anything but that. I had the chance to observe nature in a way I never could have done at my home on the mainland, which, by the way, we rented out during the summer season. I delighted in watching smallmouth black bass spawning each year near the point where the flagpole is located. The largemouth bass would spawn in the dockage area, along with the sunfish.

We watched the same turtle lay its eggs at the same place on Glen Island for two years in a row. We observed a wide variety of wildlife, including red squirrels, raccoons, ducks, chipmunks, sea gulls, frogs, countless species of birds, and the occasional harmless snake. We saw bats galore, as the cedar-shake shingle roofs of the buildings made an ideal bat habitat.

Living on an island with small children who cannot swim can sometimes be a trying experience. We spent a considerable amount of time keeping track of the kids. I recall one incident when my daughter Gail was missing for quite some time, and we were very concerned that she had perhaps fallen into the lake. After searching the island for

105

Governor Nelson Rockefeller visiting Glen Island.   © *Richard K. Dean*

hours, we finally found her sleeping on top of a picnic table in a very remote part of the island.

One year, an unidentified prankster left a large bunny rabbit on Glen Island, delighting the youngsters who came to visit. A camper from a neighboring island decided to kidnap the rabbit at one point, taking it to his island. A little detective work on the part of some campers quickly revealed who the culprit was, and the bunny was soon returned to Glen Island. However, it disappeared again shortly before Labor Day, never to be seen again.

I lived on Glen Island for 38 years on a seasonal basis, from just after ice-out in April until October, and I came to love this temporary home. I left my driftwood collection and my photographs of shipwrecks there for visitors to enjoy. I planted many trees on the island, and I hope that they will live forever-and-a-day for all to enjoy. If I had my life to live over again, I wouldn't change a thing. Glen Island and all the other Lake George islands will always be my love and joy. Since my retirement, I have made it a point to visit Glen Island every year, a tradition which I will continue to carry out until the end of my days.

PHANTOM ISLAND

PHANTOM ISLAND is a small, state-owned island located just south of Big Burnt Island. How this island got its name is a complete mystery to me. Elsa Steinback, noted Lake George artist and author, thinks that someone long ago might have thought that a ghost inhabited the island. Or perhaps, she suggests, someone lost on the lake in thick fog or during a snowstorm came upon the island suddenly, seeing it as a vague, half unreal shape.

It was on this island that J. Henry Hill, the Hermit of Lake George, lived for four years, in a cottage which he himself had built. An artist originally from Nyack, New York, Hill stayed on the island year round from 1870 to 1874. He was alone most of the time, with only his dog for company. Occasionally other artists visited, including his father, John William Hill, who also painted Adirondack scenes.

While living on the island, Hill produced several etchings and watercolors of Lake George and its islands, some of which are now in the collection of the Adirondack Museum. One of his favorite subjects was Hermit Island, located northeast of Phantom. Hill recorded his day-to-day activities on the island in a journal. In 1874, he apparently suffered a mental breakdown and was taken to an asylum, where he eventually recovered. He died in 1922 at his home in Nyack, at the age of 83.

Hill's cottage was later owned by Dr. A. W. Holden of Glens Falls, who lived on the island during the summer months. The Hon. Jerome Lapham of Glens Falls then purchased the cottage, using it as a summer retreat until the state of New York laid claim to the island in the late-nineteenth century. At that time, the state removed all the buildings. Campers from the Glens Falls area continued to camp on

Phantom Island and, in 1913, the Conservation Commission issued tent-platform permits for these campers. One of the permit holders was T. J. McGillicuddy of Glens Falls. He used campsite 1 for several years. Claire Bartlett, who lives in Bolton Landing and has a summer home on Fourteen Mile Island, remembers childhood visits to her relatives, the McGillicuddys, at their Phantom Island campsite.

Another Phantom Island camper was William Mulholland, former Superintendent of Camps and Trails and Director of Lands and Forest for the state, who pitched his tent on campsite 3 for several years during the 1930s.

Phantom Island is ideal for family camping, with four campsites and a sand beach on the north side of campsite 1. Though the beach is a small one, it is ideal for nonswimmers because of the shallow water.

My staff and I often recommended this island to families, especially those with young children. I vividly recall one child, Danny Wacks, who liked to canoe the 50 feet over to Glen Island to buy an ice cream cone at the commissary. Today Danny is the proud owner of the Timberlane property on Northwest Bay.

Another family, the Gordons, occupied campsite 3 on Phantom. Joseph, a New York City high school principal, and Tess, a teacher, always brought a maid along on their camping trips to do the cooking and "household" chores at the campsite as well as to babysit for the two Gordon children, Danny and Freddy. I guess this might be what one would call creating a home away from home at a campsite.

One of the permanent permit holders, a college professor named Devereux D. Robinson, was a rattlesnake hunter, and a very successful one at that. But it was not only the $5 bounty (which was outlawed in 1971) which interested Robinson. He considered the snakes to be a delicacy. I will never forget the time that Robinson offered me a slice of cooked rattlesnake. Not wishing to be impolite, I reluctantly accepted his offer. I must admit that, in my opinion, it is certainly no great loss that rattlesnakes are not a dietary staple here in the North Country. The taste was somewhat fishy, and I hope that I will never again have the dubious privilege of having to sample such a "delicacy."

BIG BURNT ISLAND

BIG BURNT Island, 30 acres in size, is the largest of the state-owned islands in the Narrows. Although the exact origin of the name is unknown, there is mention of a disastrous fire there in the late-nineteenth century.

The island may have gotten its name, however, from even earlier fires. In the days before Europeans settled this area, the Native Americans used to burn off old fields and forest edges for new crops. However, this slash-and-burn technique often resulted in forest fires which would burn out of control over huge areas. Perhaps the original inhabitants viewed Big Burnt Island as an ideal place to employ this technique, as they could be certain that the fire would not spread beyond the bounds of the island.

As anyone familiar with forests knows, blueberry bushes thrive in a burned-over area, producing bounty crops of berries. These berries are in abundance around campsites 5, 6, 7, 19, 20, and 26, evidence that a large fire occurred in that area. I recall many a camper picking these berries, and I was fortunate to be able to enjoy a pie or two made from them by Sophie Kaplan, who camped with her family on Big Burnt for nearly 50 years. She later purchased a house on Northwest Bay, where she stayed until her death in the spring of 1996.

Big Burnt was large enough to be the home of a variety of animals, including raccoons, squirrels, partridges, chipmunks, birds, and even an occasional deer in the off season. In 1889, Seneca Ray Stoddard wrote that semi-wild goats inhabited the island.

In the early 1900s, Evangeline Booth, daughter of William Booth, general of the Salvation Army, camped here for several summers.

In 1886, the steamship *Ganouskie* was towed to the island by its new owner, Captain G. W. Howard. Moored to the island, it served as a floating saloon for many years. A cage of rattlesnakes inside the saloon no doubt attracted many curiosity seekers. Perhaps visitors to the *Ganouskie* were even served blueberry pie for dessert. The iron mooring ring which held this boat can still be seen today near campsite 5.

Big Burnt was once the site of a strange overnight disappearance of a camper. It seems that Lisa, a teenager who had had a family quarrel with mom and pop, decided to make herself conspicuous by her absence. As twilight fell, Lisa's parents appeared on Glen Island to report that their daughter was missing. Calling into service almost all of the campers on Big Burnt, I helped organize a search party. Although we combed every foot of that island, we could not find Lisa. We even asked campers on the nearby islands if they had seen her, but still no leads.

Around midnight we called off our search, agreeing to meet early the next day and to notify the state police. About 6:30 the next morning, a camper from Uncas Island, which is just south of Big Burnt, came to Glen Island to report that a young girl had been found sleeping in an outhouse near an unoccupied campsite on Uncas.

There were many happy campers indeed when it was confirmed that the girl was Lisa, who had swum from Big Burnt to Uncas Island after the dispute with her parents. Lisa and her family camped on the island for several years after this incident, and we delighted in teasing her about her overnight disappearance.

Many lifelong friendships were sparked on this island in the days when campers could remain on a site for as long as they wished, some even staying for the entire summer. Big Burnt was considered a family island, and many of the children of those long-term campers became fast friends.

Herbert Kaplan and Beatrice Swire first met while their families were camping on Big Burnt. Both were avid canoeists and obviously had a number of other common interests. When they decided to marry, they had the blessing of their parents, who knew that this marriage would be for keeps. Today Herbert is a doctor in Denver, specializing in degenerative joint diseases. He and his wife return to Lake George in the summers, spending time on Three Brother Islands, which Beatrice's family purchased in 1950. Her cousin, Dick Swire, part owner of Three Brother Islands, spent many years camping on Big Burnt in his youth. In those days, Dick was a ring leader of many of the island pranks which were more humorous than dangerous.

The Swires and Kaplans are not the only former Big Burnt campers who now have summer homes on the lake. Joel Breslau and his sister Ruth Breslau Fine, for example, whose family spent many happy days on Big Burnt, both now own homes in Basin Bay.

One couple's love for Big Burnt was so great that they requested that, upon their death, their ashes be placed under a rock in the wooded area of what had been their favorite campsite for 50 years. And each year family members visit the site paying homage to them.

GEM ISLAND

G EM ISLAND is a state-owned island richly deserving of its name.
It truly is a gem sparkling in the waters of Lake George. It is a
tiny island, measuring only about one-third of an acre. This small size,
however, did not deter D. J. Brown of Caldwell (now the town of
Lake George) from building a cottage on it in about 1889. Nestled
just to the north is an even smaller jewel, Little Gem Island.

Gem Island is one of my favorites. Perhaps it is because of my
long-time acquaintance with Elizabeth Stone, who was a nurse at
Eddy Memorial Hospital in Troy. Bessie Stone camped on the island
for more than 40 years and even had a permanent tent platform there.
After her husband died, she continued to camp on Gem, accompanied
by Jean Valenti, a friend and schoolteacher.

Bessie brought Jean along because, although she loved camping
and she loved Gem, she was afraid to stay on the island alone
overnight. Once, when Jean had to leave, Bessie paddled over to Glen
Island in her 1929 Old Town canoe in the middle of the night simply
to be near other human beings. You can imagine our surprise when we
found her the next morning asleep in the telephone booth on Glen
Island.

During the last few years of Bessie's stay on Gem, my wife Betty
and I let her sleep on the enclosed porch at our Glen Island cabin. She
came to the island just before dark and left each morning at dawn. It
was always a pleasure to have her stay with us.

Finally old age crept up on Bessie and she reluctantly gave up her
annual camping trip. The old-time campers who had known her over
the years gave her a surprise farewell party, attended by many of her
friends from far and near. All of us who knew her were saddened to

hear of her death in 1960, but we are consoled by the thought that she is surely in Heaven smiling down upon us.

Gem Island will never be the same without Bessie. If islands could speak, Gem would surely say, "Bessie, you cared for me, you were my very best tenant." The apple tree that Bessie planted on the island still bears little green apples, the fruits of her labor and of her love for the island.

HERMIT ISLAND

THIS ISLAND was probably named for J. Henry Hill, a renowned artist who lived alone on nearby Phantom Island from 1870 to 1876 and who, owing to his solitary lifestyle, came to be known as the hermit of Lake George. During his lifetime, Hill created numerous etchings of Lake George and its islands. The island which appears more frequently than any other in these etchings is the one now known as Hermit Island.

If I were naming this island, however, I would probably call it either Shipwreck or V.I.P. Island. Why Shipwreck? It is located in the shallow Fields of Lake George which have been the scene of more boating accidents than any other part of the lake. The marina operators of Lake George can relate tales of inboards, outboards and even huge cabin cruisers which they have towed off these Fields after they ran aground. And there is undoubtedly many a skipper who regrets not having taken a bit more time to study the marine maps of Lake George before venturing into this area.

And why V.I.P. Island? From 1941 to 1983 this island was used as a retreat and hideaway for many distinguished visitors. These prominent campers included Department of Environmental Conservation commissioners and their deputies, Jim Hagerty (press secretary to Governor Thomas Dewey and later President Eisenhower), state legislators, several judges, and Governor Dewey's sons Tom and John.

When no V.I.P.s were using the island, park rangers and conservation officers would camp there to keep watch over the campsite, the gear, and supplies. And what a well-supplied campsite it was.

Much like the robber barons of the late-nineteenth century who built luxurious Great Camps in the Adirondack wilderness, the campers on this island could enjoy a rustic vacation without having to sacrifice the comforts of home. The special campsite on this island had everything one might need—including the kitchen sink. The tents were large and set up on platforms. One of these, a kitchen tent housing a gas range and gas refrigerator, had its own water supply pumped into it. The sleeping tents were equipped with Coleman lanterns and rollaway beds. We would even provide linen sheets upon request, though the only person who ever took advantage of this service was a lady who was a first-time camper.

One cool summer night in 1971 I received a call shortly before midnight asking us to come tow a boat off the Fields. When I arrived at the scene, I found a boat filled with V.I.P.s. Whether they had simply overshot their destination (Hermit Island), or perhaps consumed a few too many highballs during the course of the evening I cannot say. But I will tell you that their boat was definitely in need of immediate and major repairs.

Dignitaries the world over enjoy certain perks and those visiting Lake George were no exception. This was particularly true when the dignitaries were in a position of being able to benefit Lake George, either through political or business channels. Many decisions affecting Lake George were made on this special island. If trees could talk, I'm sure that the woods of Hermit would have some interesting stories to relate.

WATCH ISLAND

WATCH ISLAND, less than a quarter of an acre in size, is a one-campsite island owned by the state. It is located in the Narrows, east of Big Burnt. The island, often windswept, is not exactly remote, since the main channel used by the steamboats of yesteryear and the large boats of today runs between Watch Island and the east shore of the lake. The channel is also used by lake trout fishermen when the "lakers" are deep.

How deep the lake trout are swimming depends on water temperature, weather, and brightness of the day. During the warm summer months, the trout go deeper in the lake, seeking colder water. They will be found in depths ranging from 85 to 180 feet from late June throughout July and August. Good luck to all you fishermen!

The name of Watch Island derives from the fact that, in former times, hunters would station themselves here to watch for deer. In the late 1800s, when it was still legal to use dogs to pursue deer, the hunters would release their trained hunting dogs into the mountainous area south of Black Mountain, on the east shore. The dogs, eager to run, would begin tracking the deer as soon they were released. Upon catching a deer's scent, the dogs would bark, putting the watchful hunters on alert.

When being pursued, the deer's animal instinct is to break the trail and get the dog off its scent by taking to the water. The frightened animal would rush through the woods and into the lake to swim across to the opposite shore or to an island, thus becoming an easy target for the hunters waiting in boats or on Watch Island.

Prior to 1880 there were no restrictions on hunting methods or on the number of deer which could be taken. By 1886, however, the law restricted each hunter to only three deer per season. Up until 1911 it also was legal to sell wild venison. I could imagine that the old hotels along the lake used to serve venison to the guests in the days before its sale was banned. If so, perhaps some of this deer meat was delivered by hunters positioned on Watch Island.

Watch Island, along with nearby Hermit Island, also could appropriately be called Shipwreck, owing to the nearby Fields. This is an extremely shallow and rocky part of the lake which has been the undoing of many a boater who, unaware of the proper navigation channels, ran aground here. Perhaps "Watch Out!" would also be a good name for this island, as many campers familiar with the Fields have undoubtedly called out this warning to approaching boaters. I am certain that, over the years, campers on Watch Island have again and again heard the gruesome sound of a boat running aground or, at the very least, propellers scraping the rocks.

Yes, Watch Island, if you could tell what you know, you could embarrass many boaters who didn't see your nearby shoals.

FORK ISLAND

FORK ISLAND is a state-owned island located at the northeastern end of the Narrows. With its 12 campsites, this island is very popular with campers. One could say, with a little bit of imagination, that the island's shape resembles a fork, with two tongues of land reaching out into the lake, creating three coves.

Fork Island also appears on some older state maps as Kettle Island. A curious hole in the rock just a few feet north of campsite 12 is undoubtedly the source for this name. Some campers surmise that this hole is an Indian kettle, crafted by the original inhabitants of Lake George. Others have suggested that the pot hole was caused by water constantly rocking a boulder until it bored a hole in the softer rock. However, the majority believe that the retreating glacier created this and other kettles at various spots on Lake George millions of years ago.

Campsite 4, located on the tip of the peninsula on the east side of the island, is particularly popular with campers. Practically an island by itself, with water on three sides, it affords a feeling of great privacy. The disadvantage of the site, however, is that it is not sheltered and can be quite windswept at times both from the north and south.

Sites 2, 3, and 5 were once occupied by campers with permanent tent-platform permits, school teachers who remained on the island throughout the summer over a course of many years. I recall one of these three teachers who enjoyed nude sunbathing as much as he enjoyed camping. Although it would not be appropriate to divulge his name, I can tell you that he almost lost his permanent permit due to indecent exposure. After that, he promised that he would always be clad in proper attire and that his nude sunbathing days were over.

These permanent permits were issued to some campers as early as 1930, but were all canceled by the state about 1960. The state stopped issuing the permanent permits in response to a growing demand for public campsites and concern about fair and equitable treatment. Island camping had been becoming more and more popular ever since the end of World War II. By the end of the 1950s, there were no longer enough campsites to accommodate campers who wanted to stay for short periods of time. The state therefore decided to issue permits limited to a maximum two-week stay. This was a reasonable limitation at a time when the majority of the population took its vacations in two week blocks. The times had changed and the state policies also had to change.

Since there was now little incentive for the permanent-permit holders to maintain their tent platforms, these platforms deteriorated and the state removed them to avoid possible injury. Over time, the state constructed its own tent platforms on sites where the terrain was not suitable for pitching a tent. Recent statistics indicate that shorter vacations and weekend camping are increasing in popularity, with very few campers actually staying for the maximum allowed period of two weeks.

AS YOU WERE ISLAND

T HIS SMALL, state-owned island at the northern end of the island
group known as the Narrows is near Tongue Mountain on the
lake's western shore.

Most of the individual Lake George islands have a special story
connected to them, and this island is no exception. The tale of As You
Were Island—which historians think first appeared in print in 1863—
tells of an old man, a former soldier, who set out in his rowboat for a
hunting trip on the Tongue Mountain range. Luck was on his side that
day; as he approached the Narrows he saw a deer on this small island.
Picking up his flintlock rifle, the hunter took careful aim and fired.
Unfortunately, however, he missed his target. Flustered and without a
moment's thought, he shouted an old military command, "As you
were!"

As the story goes, the frightened deer was so startled that it did not
know which way to turn. It stood perfectly still while the hunter
reloaded his musket and fired again, this time felling his prey.

Today, motel and marina proprietors, cruise ship captains, and
private boat owners delight in relating this and other yarns and
legends to their guests as they tour this particularly beautiful part of
Lake George. I'm not sure who delights more in these tales, the
storytellers or the listeners.

Despite the island's tiny size (just over one-eighth of an acre), it was
used as a one-campsite island from 1920 to 1942. In 1934, the Conservation Department issued a tent platform permit to Arthur Chafetz to
erect two platforms. For the next eight years, Chafetz camped on this
island throughout most of the summer. In 1942, for environmental
reasons, the state decided to ban camping on As You Were Island.

The island is rock ledge and tends to be windswept, two factors which make it less than ideal as a camping island. In my opinion, the state was wise to prohibit both camping and day use here, and I can only hope that this prohibition will remain in effect permanently.

SARAH AND HAZEL ISLANDS AND PARADISE BAY

THE TWO state-owned islands, Sarah and Hazel, are located on the eastern shore of Lake George, at the entrance of Paradise Bay. Camping was allowed on Sarah Island until the late 1930s when it was converted to a day-use and picnic island.

How these islands got their names is not entirely clear. However, shortly after the creation of the state Forest Preserve, a commission was appointed to name the state-owned islands. I believe that Sarah and Hazel, along with Agnes Island, may have been named for daughters or wives of these commissioners, though it is not possible to confirm this since the names of the commissioners were never recorded. Commission Island was probably also named after this commission.

Beyond Sarah and Hazel Islands lies the lovely and peaceful Paradise Bay. The bay is shut off so completely from the main body of the lake by barriers of trees and rocks that visitors to the bay have a sense that they are on their own miniature lake. A narrow strip of soil and rock separates Paradise Bay from Red Rock Bay, a sheet of water to the south which rivals Paradise Bay in its beauty.

Paradise Bay is just one of the many gems which sparkle throughout Lake George. Surrounded by undeveloped state land, this scenic bay remains eternally calm, even when heavy winds whip the rest of the lake into frothy whitecaps. For its size, it is the most frequented bay on Lake George.

Elsa Steinback, Lake George artist and author, recalls hearing her mother tell of childhood trips she took with her sister each Sunday to Paradise Bay in the 1890s. The Pearl Point House, where they were staying, had a "church boat" to take guests across the lake to Bolton for church services. Guests who did not take the church boat would row or paddle to Paradise Bay. Here, surrounded by the calm tranquillity of the bay, they would sing hymns, giving them a sense of spiritual uplifting.

Because of the bay's popularity, the DEC long ago prohibited camping, picnicking, or day use on the shoreline here, a policy which continues to this day. In 1992, the Lake George Park Commission went a step further and banned boats from anchoring in the bay.

Throughout the 1980s and early 1990s, the large numbers of boats anchoring in Paradise Bay became a serious problem, creating congestion and making navigation almost impossible. The *Mohican*, a Lake George cruise boat which offers a daily trip to Paradise Bay, found that it no longer had room to maneuver in the bay. The skill required to turn this 115-foot vessel in the limited navigable waters at the entrance to Paradise Bay—a mere 180 feet in width—is so exceptional that, throughout the years, hundreds or perhaps even thousands of campers and boaters have followed the *Mohican* into the bay just to marvel at the feat. I can recall the many times I watched Tom Conerty, a former captain of the *Mohican* and now captain of the *Lac du Saint Sacrement*, as he guided his vessel into and out of Paradise Bay.

The LGPC ban on anchoring here has alleviated the crowding somewhat so that the *Mohican* can now come into the bay and do its turnaround without any problems, and visitors can once again enjoy the bay's tranquillity. I made the following statement at one of the public hearings held by the LGPC on whether or not to forbid anchoring in Paradise Bay: "Enter the bay and cruise slowly to the most southerly part. As you make your circle, look to the north and you will find yourself completely landlocked. This beauty belongs to all of us, to be shared and not monopolized. No one will ever convince me that the presence of 50 to 75 boats anchored in this relative small bay does not have any impact on the waters of Paradise Bay."

I first set eyes on Paradise Bay in 1940 and have made it a point to visit it every year since then. During the course of my employment with DEC, I observed a drastic change in the clarity of the water, as well as increased activity on the shore. However, despite these changes, the characteristics which have attracted visitors to Paradise Bay over the past century are still there. The shoreline still resembles a primeval forest, a refreshing thought in view of the many dramatic changes which have affected the shores of Lake George throughout this century.

DEC policy restricting the use of the state land in the bay as well as the LGPC restrictions on anchoring will ensure that future generations will be able to enjoy an environmentally sound Paradise Bay. My love for this bay continues to grow.

Sarah and Hazel Islands, Paradise Bay, and Red Rock Point.   © *Richard K. Dean*

HALFWAY ISLAND

H ALFWAY ISLAND is a small, state-owned island located, as its name implies, about halfway up the lake. The island is at the center of a semicircle created by a mountain which rises, amphitheater-like, on the nearby western shore. Mountain Bay, which is at the base of this mountain, is often referred to by old-timers on the lake as Amphitheater Bay.

For many years prior to 1943, the island housed a sole campsite. However, it was during that summer that a fire ravaged the island. This was my second year of employment with the state and my first major island fire. When I arrived on the scene, the fire was confined to a large tent platform on the island, near the dock.

Two factors made fighting the fire extremely difficult: The intense heat from the fire prevented us from coming in too close, and the wind whipping down the lake that day fueled the flames and dissipated the spray from our water pump. However, we did manage to get the fire under control by the time the Bolton Fire Department arrived.

At least half of the trees were burned or scorched, scarring the island's beauty. The fire was probably caused by the carelessness of a group of picnickers. After the disaster, the state immediately prohibited both camping and day use on the island, a prohibition which has remained in effect to this day.

A few years after the fire, we enlisted the aid of our Boy Scouts of America Explorer Post of Bolton to plant a large number of white and Norway pine trees on the island. Thanks to this and Mother Nature's helping hand, today no one would ever suspect that a fire had once so severely damaged the landscape.

Halfway Island's terrain is not conducive to camping, since it would be difficult to pitch a tent here or site a tent platform. It is my hope that the state will continue its prohibition against camping on or day use of this island since its particular beauty would be diminished by public use. Other islands which have been taken out of public use— and which I hope will remain so—are Sweetbriar, As You Were, Little As You Were, Chingachgook, Delaware, and Huletts.

The Harbor Islands

T HIS GROUP of five private islands is located about .75 mile north of the northernmost of the state-owned Mother Bunch group and about 2.25 miles south of Sabbath Day Point. The name derives from the fact that the group provides excellent harborage for vessels of considerable tonnage.

The largest island in the group is named after Father Isaac T. Hecker, a noted author, lecturer, and priest. A convert from Methodism, he was received into the Catholic Church in 1844 and went on to become a priest. Desiring to initiate a distinctly American approach to the priesthood, he joined three other like-minded priests in founding the Paulist Fathers in 1858. By 1868, the group had 11 priests as well as several students.

Hecker first came to the lake in the summer of 1868, bringing fellow Paulists for a retreat. They stayed with their friend Charles Sloane O'Connor, an attorney famed for his prosecution of Boss Tweed and his ring. O'Connor owned a house on the east side of the lake, about three miles north of Lake George Village. Some of the priests stayed in his home, while others camped in tents on the property. In 1872, O'Connor donated his mainland property to the Paulist Fathers, who still own it today. A residential structure was built on the property, which is known as St. Mary's of the Lake, that same year. In 1954, Arthur Mannix, a Lake George architect and contractor, erected a white pine chapel which included their makeshift altars.

While at Lake George, Father George Deshon, another one of the founders of the Paulist Fathers, encouraged the young students at Lake George to go boating and sailing. Although stern, with a voice that once barked army commands, he taught them to relax, to read,

Paulist Chapel on Hecker Island.   © *Richard K. Dean*

and to enjoy themselves. From their earliest days at Lake George, the Paulists visited the Harbor Islands, often camping there in tents. They purchased the islands from the state for $100 on December 28, 1871.

When the Paulists acquired the Harbor Islands, they retained the group name, but also named individual islands after their founders: Deshon (called Eagle by the state), Hewitt, Hecker, and Baker.

In 1906, to honor Saint Isaac Jogues, the first European to see Lake George, the Paulist Fathers built a chapel on the southeast end of Hecker Island. The chapel, perched on solid rock, is constructed of wood and plaster, with a marble crucifix on its eastern side.

The chapel was used exclusively by priests and seminarians until 1964. (The Second Vatican Council, which met from 1962 to 1965, redefined which structures could be used for celebration of masses, limiting the use of private chapels and oratories for this purpose. The Code of Canon Law was revised in 1983 to allow the celebration of masses in this type of structure under certain conditions.) Neglected over the next 30 years, this unique island chapel deteriorated until, in 1994, it caught the interest of Rev. Frank DeSiano, national president of Paulist priests. Through his efforts, money was earmarked to rehabilitate the historic chapel.

A contractor was hired to replace the roof, while teams of priests and seminarians scraped and painted the exterior of the chapel. They performed their task with enthusiasm, knowing that the chapel would once again be serving its original purpose as a place of worship. The first mass in the renovated chapel was held on August 18, 1995, after three decades of abandonment.

During their stays at Lake George, the Paulist fathers and seminarians used the kitchen and sleeping quarters on Hewitt Island. Four Paulist fathers were on the island in June 1983 when these buildings burned. They were rebuilt the following year and are today still used by the vacationing Paulists.

There is a narrow but navigable channel between Hewitt and Hecker which is known as the Needle's Eye. Pleasure-boat captains delight in "threading the needle," impressing uninitiated passengers with their skill in guiding their craft through this passage. Local photographer and publicist Walt Grishkot, who used to run sightseeing cruises in his boat named the *Black Arrow*, remembers awing his passengers when he took them under a Paulist relaxing in a hammock stretched between the two islands.

History records many acts of warfare on various Lake George islands, and the Harbor Islands are no exception. One of the lake's bloodiest battles occurred on July 5, 1757, when Colonel John Parker was camped on the Harbor Islands with over 350 English troops. They were on their way north from Fort William Henry, scouting for enemy French troops, when they were attacked by a group of French-allied Indians. It was a massacre, with only 12 of the Englishmen escaping with their lives; 131 of them were killed in the battle and the remainder were captured.

During my tenure on the lake from 1941 to 1983, 38 of those years on Glen Island, I witnessed many selfless acts by the Paulist students that were a credit to them and a contribution to the lake. They helped

A Fay and Bowen "threading the needle."   © *Richard K. Dean*

battle forest fires and they rescued swimmers. I often saw them in the
St. Paul, their 38-foot fishing boat, towing boats which had broken
down, or assisting campers in canoes who had run into rough waters.

I also remember a day more than 50 years ago when the *St. Paul*,
which had a draft of almost three feet, hit a reef off the west side of
Little Harbor Island, a state-owned island in the Narrows with no
connection to the Harbor group. Using the *Banshee*, the state boat, we
towed the *St. Paul* to Glen Island, bringing the boat and its 16
passengers to safety.

The Paulist Fathers sold the *St. Paul* in the mid-1970s. It remained
on the lake for several years thereafter, changing hands several times.
A group of scuba divers owned the vessel for a period of time, using it
as a dive boat. I am told that the *St. Paul* was later transported to a
boatyard on Long Island, where it was originally built. The man who
purchased the boat has had it refurbished and now lives on it.

VICAR'S ISLAND AND
CAPTAIN SAM PATCHIN

VICAR'S ISLAND, a state-owned island of about eight acres, is
located north of the Harbor Islands, opposite Deer's Leap. Its name
derives from a man named Vicar who lived on the island. However, it
is not known when he lived there, or whether Vicar was his first or last
name or perhaps his calling.

It is said that a fisherman once happened to be passing by the island
when he noticed a commotion on the shore. Upon landing on the
island, he discovered the son of the original inhabitant (Vicar) wild
with grief and mourning over his dead father's body.

The island was also the scene of another tragedy involving Captain
Sam Patchin. Patchin (also spelled Patchen in some accounts)
originally came to Lake George from Connecticut as a young soldier
during the Revolutionary War. He fell in love with the area and made
up his mind at that time to return later to settle.

In 1798 he built a log cabin at Sabbath Day Point, in the town of
Hague on the western shore north of Vicar's Island. Captain Sam was
a man of great physical strength and stamina and was said to be the
life of the party whenever social events were held.

He became a farmer, planting grain and transporting the harvest to
a mill at Bolton. It seems that one blustery winter day he decided to
experiment with a new method of getting the grain to Bolton.
Loading the bags onto an old cutter, he hoisted sail and set off with a
pitch fork in his hand for a rudder.

The trip did not go smoothly, as Seneca Ray Stoddard recounts in
his 1889 book entitled *Lake George*:

> The ice was glare, and the cutter sailed well—remarkably well;
> but there was not so much certainty about the satisfactory

behavior of the steering apparatus. The old man, it is said, was given to spiritual things occasionally and had, on this occasion evidently hoisted in rather too much rye in the liquid form to conduce to the safe transportation of that in the bags. The craft insisted on heading directly for the island, and could not be diverted from its course . . . He decided to jump the island—he tried it; it was not, strictly speaking a success. The cutter reached the shore, and hesitated—a part of it. Sam was anxious to get along, and continued on; then he got discouraged and paused— in a snowdrift.

Patchin survived the misadventure, though the fate of his grain is not recorded. He lived to the ripe old age of 86, passing away in Hague in 1844.

Sabbath Day Point later became the site of the Sabbath Day Point House, operated for 57 years (1899 to 1956) by the Carney family. It came into the Carney family's possession when Frank Carney, Sr., married Adele Westurn, niece of Samuel Westurn, who had first begun taking in guests in 1860. Carney enlarged the hotel and built up the surrounding 500-acre farm.

Frank and Adele had three children, Eva, Olga, and Bruce. Upon his father's death, Bruce took over the operation of the hotel. Bruce married Lillian Kelly and had three sons, Frank, Jack, and Bruce. In 1956, the Carney family sold the property to developers, and the hotel and its buildings were torn down to make way for summer and year-round homes. Frank and Jack Carney still live at Sabbath Day Point.

But let us return now to the original subject of this chapter, Vicar's Island. Popular with campers, the island today contains 11 campsites, each with dockage. It has been in the possession of the state since 1876.

Joe Rota, former supervisor of the town of Dresden and currently the executive director of the Adirondack Park Local Government Review Board, always has had a passion for this island. In fact, he and his wife were married on the island on July 1, 1971. Bolton town justice Angelo Root officiated at the ceremony.

WALTONIAN ISLAND

WALTONIAN ISLAND, a state-owned island located about one mile north of the Town of Hague's boat launching site, is the outermost and largest of a group of nine islands known as the Walton or Cook Islands.

Waltonian Island was named for the Waltonians, a sportsmen's club founded in Glens Falls in 1853. The group took its name from the English author Izaak Walton (1593–1683), who was known as the father of angling. Each summer the Waltonians would set up camp on the island, bringing with them immense tents and all the amenities necessary to ensure that wilderness camping did not become too primitive. In 1870 however, a fire of unknown cause ravaged Waltonian Island. The club moved to Phelps (now Mohican Island). The Waltonians became frequent patrons of the nearby Fourteen Mile House where they spent many evenings enjoying the dining, music, and dancing.

In the late 1890s Colonel William D'Alton Mann built a fine residence on Waltonian Island where he entertained many friends. Colonel Mann was the prosperous, if not entirely reputable, publisher of the New York magazine *Town Topics*, a publication dedicated almost exclusively to reporting on members of American high society and their scandals. The magazine became *The New Yorker* after it was sold around 1920.

Among the friends Colonel Mann entertained were the renowned New York artist Harry W. Watrous and his wife, Elizabeth. Mr. and Mrs. Watrous lived in a large house (now the Ruah Bed and Breakfast) on the mainland near Waltonian Island. Harry Watrous and Colonel Mann, both of whom had a vivid imagination and a sense of humor, delighted in trying to outdo each other's practical jokes.

Waltonian Island looking north.   © *Richard K. Dean*

In the summer of 1904, Watrous came up with a magnificent hoax
when he fashioned a sea serpent from a 10-foot-long cedar driftwood
log. He carved the head with a big mouth, a couple of donkey-like ears
and four big teeth. The monster's eyes were made of two green glass
telegraph-pole insulators. The head was painted with yellow and black
stripes, the inside of the mouth was red and the teeth were white.

Watrous attached a rope to the bottom of the log. This rope was
fed through a pulley anchored to the lake's bottom with a stone and
then on to his boathouse on the shore, from where Watrous could
manipulate the monster, making it dive and surface at will.

Watrous anchored his sea serpent close to the path which Colonel
Mann's boat would have to follow to get to his island. After testing the

contraption several times, he sunk it and waited for the unsuspecting colonel and his party to pass by the spot.

Hiding behind a clump of bushes, Watrous watched as Colonel Mann's launch approached. When it was about 10 feet away, he released the line, forcing the monster to the surface. With the passengers screaming in fear, and Colonel Mann shouting, "Good God, what is it?" Watrous immediately pulled the sea serpent down to the bottom of the lake to ensure that the group would not have a chance to examine it too closely.

By nightfall, news of the sea serpent had spread along the shore. In the weeks thereafter, Watrous stole out under the cloak of darkness, moving his monster to different sites. Everybody who saw it had a new story to tell of their frightening experience. Each day, Watrous provided new thrills for the populace, and the rumor quickly spread that there was an honest-to-goodness sea serpent living in Lake George.

The New York Sun even wrote about the monster, headlining its article: "Is there a sea serpent in Lake George?" The monster reportedly ruined the eternal bliss of one young couple honeymooning at the nearby Island Harbor House when it surfaced close to their canoe, causing it to capsize. The groom, obviously unable to keep his wits about him, swam to shore, leaving his bride to fend for herself. She made her way to shore, stormed into the hotel and packed her bags, announcing not only the end of the honeymoon but also of the marriage. The monster wreaked havoc with the tourist trade for several seasons until Watrous finally grew tired of the prank.

In 1961, Walter Grishkot, organizer of the Adirondack Balloon Festival, noted Glens Falls photographer and former summer resident of Sabbath Day Point, discovered the Lake George monster in the garage of Louis Spellman, Sr., in Silver Bay. Local newspapers reported on the resurfacing of the monster, and Kay Bailey of St. Thomas, Virgin Islands, who was vacationing in the area at the time, read the stories. She decided that she simply had to have the monster for her very own. Her cousin, Shirley Armstrong, offered Mr. Spellman $25 for the creature and presented it to Ms. Bailey as a birthday present. But before the serpent departed from the region, a farewell party was

The Lake George Monster. *Photo by Walt Grishkot*

held by the Lake George, Bolton, and Hague Chambers of Commerce. At the party, the monster was christened "George."

Over the next two years, George participated in a number of parades and carnivals in his new Caribbean home until Walt Grishkot and his wife Joan visited Ms. Bailey and convinced her that George should return to his Lake George home. Walt relates the story of the difficulties he encountered trying to get George through Customs. "The officers didn't know how to estimate the duty on George," he said, "because, in their books, there was nothing listed under the category of monster." Today, George resides at the Lake George Historical Society Museum on Canada Street, where he is on loan from Ms. Armstrong.

Colonel William Mann built Saunterer's Rest, as he called his Waltonian Island residence, in 1887 on state land. In 1899, the state recognized that the legislation it had passed in 1885, which made the island part of the Forest Preserve, required the removal of private residences. Colonel Mann, however, refused to budge. For the next 17 years he fought the state for the right to remain on the island. In 1916 the state finally forced him to remove his house from the island. When winter arrived, the house was cut into three pieces and hauled across the ice to the mainland, using oxen, jacks, and pulleys. In 1922, the colonel died and the house was sold to the Clifton family, proprietors of the nearby Island Harbor House Hotel. They used it as a guest cottage until the hotel burned in 1933 and the former Mann house was converted to the main hotel building. In 1967, the Cliftons sold the hotel to the Al Lawrence family. Today, the large white house on the point, harbored by the islands, is the summer home of the Lawrences.

Waltonian Island has seven campsites. It is a favorite with campers wishing to be close to the mainland.

During the years 1942 to 1947, one of my duties as a campsite ranger was to travel by boat to all the islands north of the Narrows to issue camping permits. In this capacity, I visited Waltonian Island, a favorite with families, at least once a week. I remember being invited for lunch by many of these campers. This was a real luxury, especially when I had not packed a lunch of my own. I particularly remember the Bernie Fitzsimons family, who often welcomed me with a huge ham, cheese, lettuce, and tomato sandwich.

Reunion of Civil War veterans, circa 1904, at the house of Colonel D'Alton Mann (center) on Waltonian Island.

PRISON ISLAND

PRISON ISLAND, which is state-owned, is Lake George's most northerly island worthy of mention. Prior to 1881 it was called Mutton Island, though its current name is surely more appropriate.

In 1758, as part of British Prime Minister William Pitt's three-pronged attack on the French, General Abercromby and his army of 15,000 men set up an encampment on the mainland just west of this island. This point became known as Howe's Point, in honor of Lord Howe, who accompanied Abercromby. It was from this site, which the French called Burnt Camp, that Montcalm had embarked the previous year on his way to attack Fort William Henry at the southern end of the lake.

From their encampment, the British staged what proved to be an ill-fated attack on Fort Ticonderoga. During the first skirmish, in which Howe was killed, the British captured 148 French prisoners and brought them to Prison Island. According to local legend, the French, who were well acquainted with this part of the lake, knew that they could easily wade ashore from the island. During the night, when all was still, they quietly waded across the channel to the mainland, thus leaving the not-so-watchful English guard in command of a deserted island. It was from this escapade that the expression "taking French leave" originated. However, it must be remembered that many such stories about Lake George history are often rooted more in lore than in fact.

Nevertheless, there is no doubt that it would have been possible in those times to wade from the island to shore. The water's depth at that point today is waist high, according to Bob Rostetter of the DEC. No one knows the shallow waters of Lake George any better than Bob,

139

who has been setting the buoys and navigation aids for DEC since 1979. But during the eighteenth century the water was even shallower. A man-made dam installed at the northern end of the lake earlier this century has raised the lake's level almost two feet.

Before the state took over ownership of the island in 1876, a private cottage had been erected here. This was later moved across the ice to Black Point, on the lake's east shore.

The state prohibits camping and picnicking on Prison Island. However, during my tenure with DEC, we generally looked the other way if campers stayed on the island for just one night, particularly if they were island-to-island campers traveling the entire length of the lake. This type of camper generally left the island as he or she had found it and was careful to extinguish completely any camp fires.

Unfortunately, there is an exception to every rule. I can recall issuing a one-night permit to a camping party of three young men who promised to move to a more southerly island the next day. About a week later, I visited Prison Island and was surprised and dismayed to find this trio still on the island. With no picnic table, no fireplace and no toilet, this island was definitely not set up for more than a one-night stay. As any seasoned camper can well imagine, the island was a disaster area after this group's one-week encampment. I remained on the island for at least two hours, using my powers of persuasion to ensure that these campers got the island back in shape.

Erosion has wreaked havoc with this island over the years. Not only the waves, but also heavy rains have caused erosion, washing sand and gravel into the lake. In 1903, Captain Elias S. Harris noted in his book, *Lake George, All About It*, that Prison Island was only about half as large as when he had first seen it approximately 60 years earlier. The most recent survey, conducted in 1918, showed a total size of just under .3 acre. If a survey were to be made again today, I am sure that it would show that the island has shrunk even more.

Thus, I was very pleased when the DEC decided in September of 1996 to rip-rap Prison Island. Rip-rapping is a process by which stones are placed along the shoreline to prevent the waves from eroding it. The work was carried out with the help of—appropriately enough—prisoners from the Moriah Shock Incarceration Facility.

Prior to 1994, Prison Island did not appear on any town tax rolls, a fact I discovered while making an inventory of which islands belonged to which townships. I brought this fact to the attention of Lake George Park Commissioner and Ticonderoga resident Gordon Burleigh, as well as then-Assemblyman James King, also a Ticonderoga resident. Actions were soon initiated to have the oversight corrected; today, Prison Island is on the tax rolls of the town of Ticonderoga.

SENECA RAY STODDARD

SENECA RAY STODDARD, born on a farm in Wilton, New York, on May 13, 1843, was a man of many talents. Although probably best known for his photography of Lake George and the Adirondack region, Stoddard also was an accomplished map maker, creating detailed maps and charts of Lake George. In addition, he was a writer of guidebooks, an illustrator, and a popular lecturer.

Stoddard first came to Glen Falls at the age of 20, supporting himself by painting signs and ornamental decoration. It was here that he began working with his stepuncle Hiram Philo, who surveyed many tracts of land around Lake George. Under Philo's tutelage, Stoddard acquired training as a civil engineer.

But Stoddard's real avocation was photography. He was fortunate in being able to combine this interest with his map-making talents. As he traveled around the Adirondacks photographing the region's wild beauty, he carefully recorded details of the landscape. Soon Stoddard began producing his own maps of the region, revising them annually to include ever more roads, rail lines, inns, hotels, townships, and other information which would be beneficial to guides, travelers, sportsmen, and hikers.

In 1872 he compiled several of his photographs as well as some of his maps into a book entitled *Lake George*. The book was not intended as a guide or a detailed history of the lake, but rather as a collection of pictures and texts which would be of interest to the casual visitor. The first book contained 11 photographs: Lake George from the south; Fort William Henry Hotel; the ruins of Fort William Henry; Tea, Recluse, and Sloop Islands; views of Bolton, the Narrows, Black Mountain, Sabbath Day Point, and the ruins of Fort Ticonderoga.

Each year thereafter, Stoddard revised the book, adding other nearby lakes and describing more and more points of interest. The guidebook was published annually until 1915 and has today become a collector's item. I am proud to have in my possession a copy of the 1889 edition.

During his lifetime, Stoddard gained considerable fame as a photographer. Some of his most famous pictures are of the old hotels which once dotted the shoreline of Lake George and other Adirondack lakes, the numerous steamboats which once plied the waters, the Great Camps, and the individuals of the Adirondacks, including illustrious guides such as Old Mountain Phelps. Today his photographs are found in several public collections, including the Adirondack Museum at Blue Mountain Lake, the Chapman Historical Museum and Crandall Public Library, both in Glens Falls; the Adirondack Community College Library in Queensbury; and many private collections. The Chapman collection is the largest, containing over 7,000 items. According to Maitland C. DeSormo, in his book *Seneca Ray Stoddard,* "By actual last count, one hundred nineteenth century authors and agencies plus at least 25 recent writers have used Stoddard's photos to enhance their own literary efforts."

In 1880, Stoddard produced a four-color map of Lake George, showing the names of property owners, locations of hotels, and detailing the steamboat routes, roads, and railroad lines. It plotted all of the lakeshore communities—Caldwell (now Lake George Village), Bolton, Dresden, Hague, Fort Ann, Putnam, and Ticonderoga. The map was approved by the New York State Engineer and Surveyor and was revised frequently until its final printing in 1915.

Both the New York State Fish Commission and the New York State Forestry Commission bought large numbers of the Stoddard maps. Stoddard's ledgers show that the Forestry Commission alone purchased 1,200 copies.

During the first decade of this century, Stoddard devoted a large amount of time to preparing a hydrographic chart of Lake George. With the help of R. J. Brown, a civil engineer from Bolton, and George Slade, city engineer of Glens Falls, thousands of soundings were painstakingly recorded. The team had helpers around the lake who assisted them in taking the deep soundings. These included Captain Lee Harris of east Lake George, Alex Taylor of Bolton, Gillette Bartlett of Sabbath Day Point, and George Cook of Baldwin. The steamboat routes were charted by steamboat captains Wesley Finkle of Bolton Landing and Walter Harris of Lake George.

The chart, five feet in length and drawn on a scale of three miles to the inch, was published in sections over the years, with the entire project finally being completed in 1910. The map, used by boaters, anglers, and campers, was invaluable in helping them steer clear of the various navigational hazards and safely reach their destination.

Stoddard died in Glens Falls in 1917 after a lengthy illness. Sadly, after his death he was largely forgotten until the middle of this century, when the June-July 1949 issue of the New York State Conservation Department magazine *The Conservationist* finally accorded him his rightful place in history. In a fitting tribute, the magazine noted:

> Any of a dozen appellations would describe Seneca Ray Stoddard
> but posterity will know him best as the man who, with his bulky,
> old-fashioned camera and tripod, his glass plates and emulsions,
> captured the Adirondacks. By recording so faithfully and with
> such feeling the beauty of the North Woods, Stoddard provided
> a powerful argument for both their protection and their
> enjoyment. He was a conservationist.

GEORGE O. KNAPP

IT WAS in 1894 that George O. Knapp, founder and first president of Union Carbide Company, first came to Lake George. While on a honeymoon with his second wife, Knapp stopped at the Hundred Island House at Shelving Rock during a tour of the lake in his rented steamboat. The hotel's owner, Reuben C. Bradley, was holding an auction of the hotel and surrounding land on that particular day. A number of prospective buyers were milling about on the grounds, prepared to offer bids. Knapp, overwhelmed by the beauty of the spot, immediately offered a bid which Bradley could not refuse and which the other bidders could not top. Before the auction even started, Bradley had sold the entire property to Knapp.

In 1910, another family settled on the lake's east shore, building a summer home on a parcel of land surrounded by the Knapp estate. It was the family of Elsa Steinback, noted artist and author of the Lake George classic, *Sweet Peas and a White Bridge*. Elsa's grandfather had been bringing his family to the nearby Pearl Point House, on the shoreline just north of Fourteen Mile Island, since 1893. When his children began presenting him with grandchildren, he decided it was time to build a place the family could call its own.

The Steinback cottage is located on the shoreline just opposite Fourteen Mile Island. Until her death in November 1996, Elsa spent every summer of her life at her beloved Shelving Rock cottage, moving to her home in Bolton Landing for the colder months. I owe Elsa a huge debt of gratitude for the wealth of information she provided me about the Shelving Rock area and its history.

During the early years of this century, Knapp added to his holdings, purchasing both wild forest land and the cleared mountain

Pearl Point. Photograph by Stoddard. *Courtesy the Chapman Historical Museum*

farms near the hotel, until his estate measured 7,600 acres, including about 10 miles of lakeshore. He purchased most of the land at $1 per acre, vowing to keep almost all of it "forever wild."

As he bought up the farms, Knapp encouraged the farmers—who had been barely eking out a living—to remain on the land rent free. He knew that he would need these able-bodied individuals to help him carry out the plans he and his wife had for developing the estate.

Mr. and Mrs. Knapp selected as their building plot a site on a slope more than 200 feet above the water's edge, directly under the Shelving Rock cliff. The main house, a massive shingled building commanding a sweeping view of the lake and its islands, was completed in 1902. Thousands of man hours were spent cutting the stone for the steps, borders and patios surrounding the house. Much of the project's stonework, which stemmed from the second point south of Commission Point, can still be seen today.

For Mrs. Knapp, who loved flowers, the workmen laid out a large garden by chiseling a shelf in the side of the mountain. Horses hauled in tons of topsoil to create a fertile bed for 181 varieties of roses. At the rear of the rose garden, a natural waterfall tumbled down over the rocks before flowing into a small brook which ran through the garden.

146

The Sayonara.   © *Richard K. Dean*

Large fruit and vegetable gardens were planted to supply the household with fresh produce. During its heyday, the estate employed somewhere in the neighborhood of 80 individuals.

To transport his guests from the Delaware & Hudson Railroad station in Lake George Village up the lake to his boathouse, Knapp commissioned construction of a yacht in 1910 which he named the *Sayonara*. This 81-foot craft with a glass-enclosed cabin was the largest privately owned steam yacht on the lake. It was later sold and, from the 1940s to the early 1970s, plied the waters of Lake George as a tour boat. Retired from service in 1973, the *Sayonara* was stored in the Knapp boathouse until it was burned (along with the boathouse) in May 1988 under a permit issued by state. The magnificent wooden boat had unfortunately deteriorated to a point where it could no longer be salvaged or restored.

Knapp designed and constructed a cable car and railroad—spanning a distance of 1,000 feet—to transport family and guests from the huge boathouse to the basement of his mountainside mansion. From there they were whisked in an elevator to the upper floors of the house.

Scores of storage batteries in the basement of the mansion, charged with power from a water-wheel generator, provided the 500,000 volts

Electric cable railway below the Big Cottage, circa 1910.

Courtesy Crandall Public Library's Center for Folklife, History and Cultural Programs (Glens Falls, NY)

needed to operate the railroad tram motor. The water power came from the Shelving Rock Brook. Because Knapp and many of his guests felt that they needed to be in constant contact with the outside world, he installed over 20 miles of telegraph line, linking the estate to the Western Union station at Glens Falls.

Knapp constructed bridle trails dotted with gazeboes, hand-laid stone retaining walls, and bridges across the Shelving Rock Brook. The trails extended from the 2,665-foot summit of Black Mountain to the top of Shelving Rock, where panoramic views of the lake could be enjoyed from the comfort of rustic gazeboes and summer houses. One gazebo, built in 1902 by Sam Taylor of Diamond Point, was later moved from the Top of the Falls to a site on the lakeshore, just opposite the north end of Fourteen Mile Island, where it still stands today.

In the barns below the Big House, 20 palomino horses and four mules were quartered. Many guests quipped that these steeds lived better than guests at the lake's many boarding houses. Knapp installed a

148

Hundred Island House. Photograph by Stoddard.   Courtesy the Chapman Historical Museum

large lantern on the gazebo atop the north-facing cliff of Shelving Rock. It illuminated automatically at nightfall, powered by acetylene gas. This guiding beacon could be seen from nearly all points on the lake.

During the off season, the Knapps divided their time between their homes in Santa Barbara, California, and Chicago. But almost every summer they returned to Shelving Rock, accompanied by an entourage which included eight maids, a butler, valet, housemen, and a chef. In addition, a staff of 30 men and 30 workhorses were kept busy maintaining the roads. From spring until the first freeze of autumn Knapp's team of house painters worked to keep the estate's buildings in good repair. Although these jobs were seasonal—at a pay of $2.50 per day plus board—Knapp also employed five families on a year-round basis as caretakers. Recognizing the value of education, Knapp hired a teacher to set up a one-room schoolhouse for the children of these families. The teacher boarded at the MacMore farm on the estate. At Thanksgiving, the Knapps always had turkeys delivered to the families.

During the cold winter months, a dozen men came in to cut 5,000 to 6,000 blocks of ice from the frozen lake for the iceboxes. The estate's icehouse was located near the shore, just south of Fourteen Mile Island. The saw used for cutting the ice is still there, near the site of the old icehouse.

I was privileged to have known three of the estate's former caretakers, as well as the present caretaker, and it is from them that I received much of the information for this chapter. Past caretakers were John Stiles (caretaker from about 1909 until 1959), Ernest Granger (1959 to 1972) and Ralph Stiles (1972 to 1990). William Walkup Jr. is the caretaker at this writing. His mother, Emma Stiles Walkup, remembers attending the one-room schoolhouse at the MacMore farm on the Knapp property.

In 1917, a faulty electrical connection set the main house on fire, burning it to the ground. Today, all that remains of the former stately structure is its massive stone foundation, almost hidden among the trees that have grown up since that time. The fire was a tragedy, consuming not only this architectural gem but all of its contents, including priceless oriental rugs and other objects of great value. Mrs. Knapp would not allow anyone to risk life or limb by venturing into the house to salvage any of the family's belongings.

Knapp built a three-story wooden structure to replace the Big House, but he rarely returned to Lake George after his wife's death in 1924. As taxes on the property began to eat away at his fortune, he decided to divest himself of some of his real estate. In 1941 he put 7,269 acres of his Lake George property—including nine miles of shoreline—on the market.

The Lake George Association lobbied the state legislature to purchase the land for just under $200,000, or about $27 an acre. Although Knapp surely could have realized a far greater profit by selling his land to developers, his decision to sell instead to the state guaranteed that it would become part of the Adirondack Forest Preserve and thus remain forever wild. The state has put a small portion of these nine miles of shoreline to use as recreational areas for all to enjoy. Commission Point is a day-use area, while Red Rock Bay provides dockage for 30 cruiser campsites. On the west side of Red Rock Point the state has established eight campsites.

When George Knapp died in July 1945 at the age of 92, his son William inherited a large fortune, including the remaining Lake George property. Upon William's death, the property passed to his children—Owen Knapp, Sally Knapp Sprole, and Anna Knapp Chapman. In 1974, the family sold an additional 225 acres of land— including a mile-and-a-half of shoreline—to the Nature Conservancy which subsequently sold it to the state in 1977 for $700,000, or about $3,110 per acre. Thus, in all, the state had acquired a total of about 10 miles of shoreline from the Knapp estate. This pristine expanse of shoreline (which includes Paradise Bay) stretches all the way from Shelving Rock Brook north to Black Mountain, interrupted only by the Steinback parcel and a short stretch of lakefront retained by the Knapps.

Sites on the property include the ruins of the mansion, bridle trails, the carriage road, the Shelving Rock gazebo, and last, but not least, Shelving Rock Falls. In former times, the Knapps were gracious in allowing hikers to explore these sites. Unfortunately, not all of those who utilized the property were considerate guests. Unauthorized camping and campfires, along with thoughtless littering, became an ever-increasing problem until the family finally decided in the early 1990s to post the entire property against trespassing.

The Knapps have always been particularly concerned about fire on the property—and with good reason. Not only did the family lose its original home to a fire, but an even greater tragedy occurred in the early years of this century when the captain of the family's boat fleet (consisting of the *Sayonara* and the *Whippoorwill*) met an untimely death. The captain, Oliver Butterfield, died from a heart attack when he and other Knapp employees were battling a forest fire near Paradise Bay.

Although Owen Knapp and Anna Knapp Chapman have now passed away, but Sally Knapp Sprole and Owen's wife, Martha Knapp, own homes on the property where they, their children, and grandchildren return each summer to vacation on the shores of Lake George.

John Apperson at work with his camera, circa 1950s.

Courtesy the Adirondack Research Library of the Association for the Protection of the Adirondacks

JOHN S. APPERSON

JOHN S. APPERSON, Lake George environmentalist and advocate, probably did more to preserve the lake as we know it than any other individual. Born in rural Virginia in 1879, he developed an interest in the outdoors and the environment at an early age. In 1900, he moved to Schenectady to take a job at General Electric. Starting at the bottom, he worked his way up the corporate ladder during his nearly 50 years with the company. He became an engineer and a manager, and ultimately rose to the position of manager of the Power and Mining Department before retiring in 1946.

As an avid outdoorsman, Apperson enjoyed camping, hiking, skiing, and canoeing. He developed a keen knowledge of the environment and exhibited a growing concern for the state Forest Preserve, which had been established by an act of the state legislature in 1885. He devoted much of his life to defending the strict application of the "forever wild" clause of the state constitution, approved in 1894, which states that all lands within the Forest Preserve must remain unchanged by man.

Appy, as he was called by his friends, made several canoe trips on Lake George during the years 1900 to 1905. He was so impressed by the natural beauty of the lake, its islands, and mountains, that he began coming to the lake every week throughout the entire year. He delighted in the lake's splendor and its changing faces in each of the four seasons.

Over the next 50 years, Apperson's dedication to preserving the Lake George basin was unparalleled. He never married, often telling friends that Lake George was his wife and its islands were his children. Somewhat of a loner, Apperson seemed to thrive on controversy. Although he antagonized many individuals over the years, his willingness to fight for what he believed in played a tremendous role in the lake's conservation, and in the end earned him the respect he so justly deserved.

One of his labors of love for the lake and its islands was his rip-rapping projects. He began in 1909 placing protective stone barriers along the shores of the islands to prevent erosion caused by waves and high water. Although Apperson carried out much of the work single-handedly, he also enlisted the aid of campers, teaching them how to rip-rap the shores of "their" islands. It was not until 1917 that the state finally agreed to support these efforts, appropriating $10,000 for the project. The previous summer, Apperson had received some funding from a private source when he convinced the Delaware & Hudson Railroad, operator of a steamboat line on the lake, to help fund the project.

Apperson acted as an unofficial superintendent for the state's rip-rapping operations, contributing a boat and a barge, as well as an immense measure of his own time and energy. His efforts enabled the state funding to go even further, significantly slowing the process of erosion on most of the lake's islands. Altogether, he was personally responsible for rip-rapping parts of 50 islands. In addition, Apperson was able to persuade many other individuals to help in the effort to protect the lake's scenic islands.

I have a photograph of several Campfire Girls, taken in 1919 on a wooden barge named *Article VII, Section 7*, hauling rocks to rip-rap the islands. I have no doubt that Apperson, at least in part, was the inspiration for these young girls to do their part to preserve the lake.

Although there was a long lapse thereafter in state funding of rip-rapping, the legislature did appropriate $38,000 for it in the early 1950s. Many Bolton residents were hired at that time, creating additional seasonal employment. Although the state's early rip-rapping projects—from 1917 to 1920—were done during the winter, with horses dragging large stones across the ice on plank sleds, the later projects were carried out during the summer months, using barges. I am a firm believer in the necessity of rip-rapping many of the islands.

Dome Island and Prison Island are two which have been rip-rapped in recent years through a combination of state and private efforts.

Another "environmental project" of Apperson's was French Point, which was owned by his employer, General Electric. The company allowed its employees to camp there on tent platforms with portable canvas-covered frames. It was Apperson who first began a subscription campaign to purchase the land from General Electric as a memorial to the environmental philanthropist George Foster Peabody. Peabody had, in the early part of this century, donated large tracts of land in the Lake George basin to the state. This included Prospect Mountain,

Rip-rapping Big Burnt Island (1917), Jay Taylor, foreman.

Courtesy the Adirondack Research Library of the Association for the Protection of the Adirondacks

overlooking Lake George, as well as what is today Hearthstone Park, one of two state campgrounds on the lake's shore. Through Apperson's efforts, and in line with the company's corporate policy of public service, General Electric agreed to sell French Point to the state in 1939 at a fraction of its market value. A plaque at the northeast end of French Point commemorates the state purchase of the land in memory of Peabody. A duplicate plaque is on display in the Bolton Museum.

But this was not Apperson's only contribution to French Point. He was also responsible for planting numerous white and Norway pines on the point, reforesting the area where the old Sherman House Hotel once stood. Today these trees are well over half a century in age and blend in perfectly with the wild beauty of the landscape.

Apperson led the fight to force squatters off the state-owned islands. A state law passed in 1885 made it illegal for anyone to have a permanent structure on state land within the Adirondack Park. However, until the second decade of this century the state had been somewhat lax in enforcing this provision. Apperson assisted the state, under Conservation Commissioner George D. Pratt, by supplying evidence of illegal occupancy. In light of this, Appy was not held in high esteem by the locals, many of whom had camps of their own on state land. To make matters worse, when a fire destroyed Henry Durrin's camp on French Point Mountain Hollow, the rumor quickly spread that Apperson was responsible. Durrin, revered by many Boltonians as an excellent hunter, trapper, and fisherman, was extremely popular. It is said that Apperson, for a period of time thereafter, feared for his life. However, in all fairness, it was never proved that he was actually the culprit.

Apperson's conservation efforts brought him into contact with several governors, including Alfred E. Smith, Franklin D. Roosevelt, and Herbert Lehman. It is reported that when the state was planning to build a road from Bolton Landing to Hague, running along the shores of the lake, Apperson took Governor Smith out in his boat to show him first hand the beauty and tranquillity of that portion of the lake. Apperson proposed an alternate route farther inland, traversing the western side of the Tongue Mountain range. A dramatic confrontation between the Superintendent of Public Works and Apperson ensued, with the governor looking on. Apperson's detailed knowledge of the state's proposal and his persuasive appeal for the inland route won the governor over. I shudder to think what that portion of the lake's shores would look like today if Route 9N had been blasted out of the rocky landscape. Furthermore, anyone who has ever enjoyed a peaceful cruise through the Narrows, passing by miles and miles of unspoiled splendor, would be hard pressed to picture that same shoreline marred by hundreds upon hundreds of noisy trucks and cars whizzing by.

Another area of concern for Apperson was the high water levels of the lake which were seriously damaging the islands. He pointed out that the level of Lake George was artificial, created by the blasting away of the natural stone dam at the lake's northern outlet in Ticonderoga and its replacement with a man-made dam.

I first met John Apperson in 1943 when, as part of my job, I was instructed to ferry him to any state-owned island that he desired. When I arrived to pick him up in the state boat, the *Banshee*, he was waiting with a group of soil scientists. I'll never forget his look of apprehension when he first saw me. I was only 24 years old at the time, and it was obvious that Apperson had some reservations about my abilities to pilot the boat safely. Before climbing aboard, he put me through a rigorous line of questioning to determine my familiarity with the islands and shoals of the lake.

Apparently he was satisfied that I would be able to deliver him and his passengers safely to our destination, namely Prison Island, the northernmost island on the lake. As we traveled up the lake, we stopped at several islands, where the soil scientists took borings in trees on the shoreline. The purpose of the borings was to determine the annual growth rate of the trees by measuring the distance between the rings. Larger spaces between the rings indicated good growth while smaller spaces indicated poor growth. The scientists also obtained water-level readings from the U. S. Geological Survey gauge at Roger's Rock, where daily readings have been recorded since the gauge's

157

installation in July of 1913. By comparing the average lake level for a particular year with the growth rate of the shoreline trees in that year, the scientists were able to determine that low water levels led to healthy tree growth, while high water levels stunted the growth.

Apperson used this data to argue his case in the courts that the water level had a significant environmental impact. Despite the data, however, the New York State Supreme Court, the Appellate Division, and the Court of Appeals all held that the water levels adopted were fair and practical. After 15 years of litigation, the final ruling by the courts was that the levels recommended by the Joint Legislative Committee on Water Levels, enacted into law in 1957, must be accepted.

Apperson was not completely alone in his efforts to preserve the lake and its islands. Nobel Prize-winner Dr. Irving Langmuir, a fellow General Electric employee, was a close friend of Apperson's and assisted him in his endeavors. Langmuir had a summer home on Crown Island, located just east of Green Island.

In 1939, when Apperson learned that Dome Island was to be sold to a developer for private campsites, he promptly conferred with Langmuir. The two agreed to purchase the island for $46,000. Apperson, who later bought out Langmuir's interest, was willing to allow camping and picnicking on the island on the condition that there would be no campfires. In 1956, he donated Dome Island to the Northeastern New York Chapter of the Nature Conservancy to perpetuate it forever as a nature preserve. The land-trust group raised $20,000 to create an endowment to protect and maintain the island and to promote its educational and scientific use.

My relationship with John Apperson continued until his death in 1964 at the age of 84. Over the years that I knew him, I remember that he was continuously photographing dead trees, trees leaning into the water along the shoreline, and shoreline erosion caused by high water levels and the lack of rip-rapping. He was persistent in his efforts to convince the state of the need for more rip-rapping.

Apperson owned a Chris-Craft inboard, aptly named *Art. XIV, Sec. 1*. It was the first Chris-Craft on Lake George, launched here in 1927.

Dr. and Mrs. Irving Langmuir, canoeing rocks to the Dollar Islands, 1910.
Photograph by Apperson.　　　　　　　　　　　*Courtesy of the Lake George Association*

I can assure you that I always took notice when his boat appeared in the Narrows. I wanted to be one step ahead of him, ensuring that dead and fallen trees in the lake were removed from state shorelines as expeditiously as possible to avoid his wrath. At times, my relationship with him was somewhat less than cordial since my loyalty was naturally to the state as my employer, and Apperson viewed the state as his adversary.

Although John Apperson was unpopular with many of his contemporaries, today's residents and tourists alike owe him a huge debt of gratitude for his willingness to devote his life to the preservation of Lake George. Owing in no small measure to his efforts, the natural beauty of the lake has been maintained. In my opinion, Apperson's countless positive actions outweighed his sometimes negative methods.

Thomas Dewey and Richard Nixon.   © *Richard K. Dean*

The Governors' Convention
at the Sagamore

Lake George and Bolton Landing were front-page news all over the United States in the summer of 1954, when the 46th Annual Governors' Conference was held at the Sagamore Hotel on Green Island from July 11 to 14.

Over 300 individuals, including the governors of 48 states, their wives, and staff members were in attendance. The press pool consisted of 97 representatives of newspapers, wire services, and radio stations from across the country. There was no television coverage of the event, since that industry was still in its infancy in those days.

The list of reporters read like a who's who in the American media— names like Jack Bell of the Associated Press; William Lawrence, Leo Egan, and John Oakes of the *New York Times*; Richard Harkness of NBC; and Gould Lincoln of the *Washington Sun*, to name but a few.

Our own local photographers, Richard Dean and Bob Edwards, were also on hand, along with Bernie Degan of the *Glens Falls Times*, and Arthur Irving of the *Glens Falls Times* and *Post-Star*. A special Western Union office was set up to handle the reports being filed by the journalists. Most of the radio commentators broadcast directly from the Sagamore, often several times a day.

Although President Dwight D. Eisenhower originally was scheduled to attend, the sudden death of his sister-in-law, Mrs. Milton Eisenhower, necessitated a change in his plans. Instead, Vice President Richard M. Nixon delivered the keynote address, speaking from notes that President Eisenhower had prepared.

In his speech, which focused on transportation, Nixon proposed a scheme for highway projects which would pay for themselves either through tolls or increased gasoline tax revenues. Perhaps Thomas

Dewey, governor of New York from 1942 to 1954, was taking notes. It was during his term that the New York State Thruway, a toll road running from New York City to Buffalo, became a reality. In later years, the toll-free Northway was constructed, linking the Thruway in Albany to Montreal.

During the conference, the governors touched on many of the same topics which are still being debated today, such as care for the elderly, gasoline and fuel taxes, unemployment, federal income taxes, and the nation's prosperity.

The conference gave New York State and the Lake George region an opportunity to present themselves in their best light to the visiting dignitaries. Governor Dewey surely played a major role in the decision to bring the conference to Bolton Landing, promoting the state and the Sagamore Hotel as the ideal venue for it. It was indeed fortunate for the region, bringing publicity which no amount of money could ever buy.

However, from my perspective as a state employee, I cannot recall that Governor Dewey ever showed any particular interest in Lake George during his tenure. The only contact which I had with the family in the years before—or, for that matter, after—the conference was when I escorted his sons, Tom and John, on an island camping trip in 1945 ferrying them in the state boat, the *Banshee*.

Associated Industries of New York ensured that the governors were made well aware of New York State products, presenting each with a tackle box, silver bracelet, Kodak camera, a pair of slippers, sunglasses, candy, aluminum bowls, gloves, an electric shaver, a bone pocketknife, a belt and buckle set, wall clock, desk thermometer, champagne, portable radio, Arrow shirts, record albums, neckties, and New York State wine.

Each governor received an ashtray specially designed and produced by the ceramics department of Alfred University and autographed by Governor Dewey. The governors' wives also received gifts which included gloves, jewelry, coin purses, perfume, scarves, and compacts.

An entire fleet of 48 brand-new, blue-and-yellow Ford sedans was brought to Bolton Landing. Each car had the name of a governor on the license plate and each had a state police officer assigned as the driver. After the convention, the cars became the property of the New York State Police.

F. J. McGinnis, the CEO of Ford Motor Company, presented the cars to the governors for their use during their four-day stay. They were parked on the Bolton Central School ballfield during the conference, attracting hundreds of interested spectators. Don Snyder, now a member of the Bolton town board and owner of a service station, remembers washing all 48 cars every day, a service paid for by the Ford Motor Company.

At the time of the conference, Jane Gabriels and her two children were spending the summer at the family home on Green Island, with the other family members arriving on the weekends. Commissioner John A. MacCormack asked Jane's father, Peter D. Kiernan of Albany, if some entertainers could be housed at the estate during the conference. Mr. Kiernan graciously offered the use of the two small houses on the property to put up the Demarco Dance Company, Tony Martin, and an opera singer.

Jane Gabriels also played hostess to Albin S. Johnson, superintendent of the state police and a friend of the family. She recalls taking him, some of his friends, and members of the press for boat rides in her father's GarWood boat, the *Black Swan*.

All of the motels for miles around were filled either with members of the press corps or state policemen. Although the conference lasted only four days, the security forces were in town for several days before and after, and security was tight throughout the conference. The state police patrolled the island and the surrounding waters day and night. Having only one point of access to the island—the bridge—made the job somewhat easier.

But it was not only the motels which profited from the conference. Restaurants and other establishments were filled with visitors who did not have the proper credentials to attend the nightly entertainment at the Sagamore.

In my capacity as the ranger for the Lake George islands, I was directly involved in the conference. My job was to take the governors fishing or on sight-seeing tours of the lake, during which we were to show the visitors that New York State, and Lake George in particular, had a lot more to offer than just politics.

We accomplished our mission, proving to the distinguished guests that the lake was rich not only in scenic beauty but also in its supply of fish. During the four days, seven governors caught a total of 17 lake trout weighing a total of 75 pounds.

Governor John Fine of Pennsylvania caught the biggest one, an 8.5 pounder. Governors Goodwin Knight of California, J. Caleb Boggs of Delaware, Edward Arn of Kansas, Lawrence Weatherby of Kentucky, Theodore McKeldin of Maryland, and J. Bracken Lee of Utah were the other fishermen of the group. A number of local men also served as fishing guides for the governors. These included Frank Dagles, Charles Peer and Ron Hill, all of whom worked for F. R. Smith and Sons marina.

The game protectors took the necessary precautions to ensure that none of the governors returned from a fishing trip empty handed. Early each morning, before anyone else was up, these game protectors went out on their own fishing expeditions, catching a number of lake trout, which they kept as a reserve. Thus, even though some of the governors caught no fish at all, they could nevertheless proudly display a few prize lake trout when they returned to the Sagamore dock to be greeted by their wives.

I have often wondered whether or not they told their wives and colleagues that the trout actually had been caught before they themselves had even gotten out of bed. It occurred to me that there is little difference between a politician and a fisherman: They both seem to love fish stories!

The detail to which I was assigned, consisting of five game protectors (Maynard Ryther, Murray Crannell, Don Bain, Charles Doody, and district game protector Francis DeCennois, who was in charge of our detail) and myself, was stationed at the house of Louis Brandt (then the owner of the Sagamore) on Green Island, awaiting requests for our services. We took many of the governors and their families on boat rides, impressing all of them with the beauty of the lake.

I remember chauffeuring Governor Theodore McKeldin of Maryland and Governor Walter Kohler of Wisconsin. Governor McKeldin gave me a rosary with beads made of olive pits as a token of his appreciation, while Governor Kohler gave me a tie clasp. He told me that Wisconsin has hundred of lakes, many of them larger than Lake George, but none as beautiful.

Carl McCoy of Lake George, director and coordinator of the Warren County Mutual Aid Fire System, was in charge of fire protection. Modern radio communication equipment, along with walkie-talkies, a 1,500-kilowatt generator, fire-fighting apparatus, and an 85-foot aerial ladder were all part of the fire-safety system. Bolton Fire Chief Arthur French, Captain Ken Palmer, and a large number of other volunteer firemen were on hand to ensure round-the-clock protection and to resolve any emergency which might arise. Fortunately, none did.

Mrs. Anita Kennedy McGilvray of Bolton Landing was assigned as the county nurse responsible for working with the firemen at the hotel. Mrs. McGilvray's many suggestions concerning which first-aid equipment should be on hand were invaluable.

Our Bolton Central School marching band marched in a parade held in honor of Vice President Nixon and the governors. I can recall the vice president making some very complimentary remarks about the band's performance. Nixon later sent a letter to Fred Dorr, music director and band leader, heaping words of praise on Dorr and the band.

I would be remiss if I did not mention other individuals intimately involved in the conference. These included photographer Bob Edwards, of Bolton Landing, who shot hundreds of pictures, and Alton Pratt, also of Bolton Landing, who tended bar at the hotel. An Edwards photograph of Vice President Nixon teeing off at the Sagamore Golf Course still hangs in the Algonquin Restaurant today.

Brandt, as owner of the Sagamore, made extensive improvements to the grounds and the hotel prior to the conference. The hotel lounge was remodeled, with one end partitioned off for use as a card room. The walls of the lounge were hung with huge scenes of Lake George.

New wall-to-wall carpeting was laid in the lounge, and many of the other rooms and the dining room were refurbished. A new television lounge, replete with air conditioning, was added. Outside, groundskeepers worked long hours to make sure that the grounds looked their very best. Many of the guests commented on the beauty of the landscaping, and in particular the lovely flower beds.

Brandt also won praise from the Federal Bureau of Investigation for his cooperation with the security forces, ensuring that security was top notch during the conference. Because President Eisenhower was originally scheduled to participate in the conference, the FBI earlier inspected all of the buildings on Green Island. Every one of the 260 staff members employed by Brandt had to be approved by the FBI. This meant that each of them had to fill out three forms, all of which were sent first to Albany and then to Washington, D. C., for approval.

The convention was truly the affair of the century for our little town. It will be remembered as the event which brought unparalleled publicity to the region, as the eyes of the nation were focused on Bolton Landing and Lake George for those four glorious days in July of 1954.

SECTION FOUR

CAMPING ON LAKE GEORGE

FOR THE CENTURIES prior to the arrival of Europeans, Lake George knew only the paddle splash of the Indian canoe. This beautiful lake was used by various Native American tribes, including the Iroquois and the Algonquins, as a transportation route as well as for hunting and fishing. At that time, Lake George camping was not a recreational activity but rather a way of life. The Indians undoubtedly slept under their bark canoes, using spruce boughs for beds, furs for blankets, and moss for pillows.

Probably the earliest people to know Lake George were the hunter tribes of the Algonquins, who were later driven out by the Iroquois. The Mohawks found the lake an excellent source of fish, which they dried and carried back to their permanent homes along the Mohawk River.

This lake, which was known at that time as *An-Di-A-Ta-Roc-Te*, meaning "the lake that shuts itself in," was a haven for these tribes until Europeans appeared in 1646. During colonial and revolutionary times, the French and the English camped on Lake George, waging fierce battles in an attempt to gain control of this important transportation route.

Peace was finally restored to the region in the late eighteenth century after decades of battles during the French and Indian Wars and the American Revolution. It was not until the end of the next century that island camping became a popular form of recreation on Lake George. Seneca Ray Stoddard, noted historian, photographer, guidebook author, and mapmaker, estimated that at least 1,000 people camped annually on Lake George during the 1880s and '90s.

Stoddard, himself a camper, recommended that the camp outfit include a light ax, long-handled frying pan, a tin pail for water or

167

coffee, tin plates, knives and forks, and fishing tackle. A fireplace, he noted, could be made of stones and mud with an old stove top laid on the top. For sleeping, a rubber blanket on the ground with two or three woolen blankets for covering would provide a camper with comfort. Flannel or woolen clothing, roomy shoes, and a soft felt hat would be the safest dress, he added. Stoddard also suggested that the women should take a man along to run errands and remove fish from the hook.

Rowboats, canoes and steam-powered boats—both large and small—were the transportation of the day. Provisions, including bacon, salt pork, bread and butter, tea, coffee, salt, and pepper could be obtained at almost any of the hotels along the lake, while milk could be purchased from local farmers. Ice, considered a luxury, was delivered by the steamships which sailed regular routes on the lake. As the steamship passed near an island where a camper had ordered ice, the ice was dumped overboard. The camper then rowed out to retrieve it, storing it in a makeshift icebox consisting of a hole in the ground covered by a piece of bark.

The weather extremes on Lake George could quickly turn a pleasant stay into a nightmare. While a shanty made of boughs might seem like a rustic romantic shelter on a hot, dry summer day, anyone stuck for three or four days in this type of makeshift dwelling while a chilly northeaster blew and dumped its torrential rains would certainly think otherwise. To make the camp more watertight, Stoddard recommended pitching a tent on a simple wooden platform which, he pointed out, could be made with little expenditure of time and money.

Even before island camping came into vogue, many tourists had already discovered the attraction of summering on Lake George. In the middle of the nineteenth century, the state started leasing or selling islands for private summer residences. Between 1855 and 1861 the state sold several islands, including Dome, Clay, Crown, Turtle, Oahu, Leontine, Fourteen Mile Island, Three Brother, Diamond, Hiawatha, Tea, Recluse, the Canoe Islands, Turtle, Hecker, Hewitt and Eagle, for prices ranging from $10 to $100. By the time the 1876 law prohibiting the sale of state land within the Forest Preserve was passed, a total of 30 islands had been sold by the state. In later years, the state acquired or reacquired Long, Speaker Heck, Turtle, and Diamond Islands by purchasing them from their owners.

In 1885, a new law gave individuals the right to act as custodians of certain state-owned islands on Lake George. A number of these individuals invested considerable time and money in beautifying "their" islands, building cottages, camps, or tent platforms in good faith on islands actually owned by the state. These included Sweetbriar, Hen & Chickens, Ranger, Uncas, Phantom, Gem, Mohican, Glen, Waltonian, Phelps, and Juanita.

It was not until 1899 that the state realized that, under the constitution, private cottages could not be permitted on state-owned islands. Suddenly, the occupants of state-owned islands were squatters. Nothing was done, however, until 1915, when a constitutional convention brought the issue of illegal occupancy of state land before the public eye. Over the next few years, most of the camps and cottages were removed either by the state or by the individuals who had built them, though a state survey in 1918 showed that a few of the camps still remained.

During the early years of this century, individuals could obtain from the local warden or forest ranger a permit to camp on state islands. The permits were for tent camping or for portable canvas houses set on permanent or temporary wooden platforms. Individuals wishing to erect a permanent tent platform could do so after obtaining special permits. However, these platforms were the property of the state and could be used by other campers. Thus, even though an individual had built his own tent platform, he sometimes had to turn it over to other campers if no other sites were available.

The popularity of island camping increased greatly during the 1920s. The New York State Conservation Commission (the forerunner of the DEC) established a headquarters on Glen Island from where it could administer the some 50 island campsites, most of which were in the Narrows. The first ranger in charge of the Glen Island headquarters was Jay Taylor, who was appointed in 1921.

It was at this time that the state began providing picnic tables and outhouses on the islands. Fireplaces, however, were first constructed by the state beginning in 1946.

The importance of sanitary regulations for the islands was first emphasized in a 1923 Conservation Commission circular. Sanitation was deemed even more important on the islands than at campgrounds elsewhere in the state. With the limited space on each island, the commission noted, refuse could quickly become objectionable. Yet, on the other hand, it was important to ensure that trash not be disposed of in the lake, the only source of drinking water.

Refuse, including tin cans, was burned wherever possible. The residual refuse was buried in holes on the island. Campers were required to keep the campsite and surrounding area clean and neat, and all items of personal property had to be removed at the end of the stay.

Other regulations required that campers bring an ample supply of lime for the pit privies. Because the islands have little soil, it was important to take every precaution to ensure that sewage be kept from draining into the lake.

As camping continued to grow in popularity during the 1930s, the state found it necessary to limit the length of stay to six weeks. New rules and regulations were adopted prohibiting the issuance of any permanent tent platform permits except in cases where rock or other topographic conditions made it impossible to stake down a tent.

From 1941 to 1945, the number of island campers dwindled as war-time gasoline rationing made it difficult for people to travel. Additionally, many of the former campers were now engaged directly or indirectly in the war effort.

In the years following the war, however, campers returned to the islands in droves. Gasoline was once again plentiful, as were boats, canoes, and sailboats, luxury items which were not manufactured during the war. Many veterans brought their growing families to Lake George to enjoy the peace and tranquillity of the islands. During these years, the state legislature appropriated funds for campsite development and renovation of existing facilities. In 1949, the state began developing Long Island—which it had purchased in

1945—eventually adding 86 campsites to the state roster. The Long Island ranger headquarters officially opened in 1950.

Another island camping headquarters had been established on Cooper's Island in 1947. This headquarters served all islands north of the Floating Battery Group and was particularly convenient for those wishing to camp on one of the Mother Bunch islands.

Prior to the establishment of the Cooper's Island headquarters, campers had to travel to Glen Island, four and a half miles to the south, to obtain camping permits. The presence of two rangers in the area also made it easier to enforce the rules and regulations on the islands.

Until 1952, camping in New York State was free. In that year, the state established a nominal fee of 50 cents per night or $3 per week for all public campsites in an effort to ensure that the services, at least in part, were paid for by those individuals who actually benefited from them. The state also pointed out that approximately 20 percent of campsite users were out-of-state visitors who, of course, paid no state taxes.

By the late 1950s, island camping was undergoing major changes. The length of the camping permit was reduced to four weeks, campsites were outfitted with new, rustic-style picnic tables, additional outhouses were erected, and fireplaces were built.

In 1956, the state, using government surplus barges, started picking up tin cans and bottles from the camping islands in the Narrows. Prior to that time, this trash was picked up only on small islands where the soil was too shallow to allow burial of the debris. By the 1950s, the trash had become a problem: Raccoons were swimming to the islands, digging up the buried tin cans and garbage, and creating an unsightly mess. The first garbage pickup crew consisted of J. Buckley Bryan Jr., Wyman Russell, and Sam Snyder of Bolton Landing. Bryan later served as president of the Lake George Association.

In later years, the department expanded its trash pickup to other islands, continuing to provide this service until 1991. Today, campers are required to bring their trash to one of the central garbage and recycling centers located on Uncas, Narrow, and Long Islands.

171

In 1959, the Cooper's Island headquarters was transferred to Narrow Island, about 300 feet off Fredericks Point in Huletts Landing. This change was made not only for the convenience of campers using the Mother Bunch and islands farther north, many of whom launched or rented their boats at Huletts, but also for administrative reasons, since the island's proximity to shore meant that telephone and electricity could be provided at a more reasonable rate.

During the late 1960s the department developed a new policy pertaining to permanent tent platforms. No new permits were to be issued and existing platforms were to be gradually phased out.

It was during this era, too, that the length of occupancy for campsites was reduced from four to two weeks. (Long Island and the Mother Bunch islands were exceptions to this rule. Campers on these islands could remain for four weeks.) With this new restriction, most remaining holders of permanent permits lost interest in maintaining their platforms.

Many of the former "permanent" campers were school teachers or lawyers from the major metropolitan areas. During the years when they were permitted to camp for extended periods, they often had at least two—and sometimes four—tent platforms, measuring as much as 14 by 18 feet in size, and framed with boards up to three feet high on the sides. They furnished their tents with beds, dressers, baby cribs, ice boxes, and sinks supplied with water pumped by hand from the lake. Many of the families brought maids or babysitters along. It was a rather luxurious form of camping. As the permanent permits were phased out and campers arrived for shorter and shorter stays, the entire face of camping on Lake George changed.

The state began, in 1958, to build its own tent platforms and docks on the islands. That first year, a total of 10 platforms and docks were constructed, with more being added each year.

In 1963 the Conservation Department purchased half an acre of land and a boathouse on Green Island, where it established an administrative headquarters and maintenance center for all island activities, including camping, day-use and installation and

ENCON headquarters on Green Island.

maintenance of navigation aids. I was very proud when, upon my retirement in 1983, the headquarters was named in my honor.

LeRoy Ryder is now the supervisor in charge of operations at the Green Island headquarters. The DEC marina there consists of boathouses, docks, storage buildings, and a marine shop with three full-time marine mechanics to take care of the DEC's 32 boats and barges as well as to service boats of other state agencies, including the Lake George Park Commission. The supervisor of the marina from 1964 to 1986 was William Lockhart. Louis Burgess served in the position from 1986 to 1994. Currently, Laverne French is in charge.

As of this writing, the state has a total of 331 individual campsites located on some 49 islands, as well as 25 additional campsites on Red Rock Point and Black Mountain shore on the mainland. An additional 42 cruiser campsites are located in Red Rock Bay and at Log Bay Island, bringing the total to 398. There are approximately 350 portable docks which are installed each spring and removed each fall

Typical island campsite on Lake George.   © *Richard K. Dean*

at the end of the camping season.

Sanitary facilities for the campsites and day-use areas include 363 pit privies, 42 tank-type toilets, and nine composting toilets. The tank privies are used in locations where only a thin layer of soil is present, or where there is clay or bare rock.

The tank privies must be pumped about four times per season. The sewage is pumped from the tank privies directly to a barge which has two holding tanks. In addition to the sewage pump, the barge contains a second pump which is used to pump fresh lake water to the tanks for clean up. This eliminates any odor and keeps the tanks sanitary. The barge then transports the sewage to Green Island headquarters where it is loaded onto a truck and hauled to a DEC-approved sewage disposal area.

There are approximately 650 picnic tables and 257 tent platforms on the various islands and day-use areas. Long Island headquarters has jurisdiction over 90 campsites and 58 day-use sites; Narrow Island headquarters administers 96 campsites and 12 day-use sites; and Glen Island headquarters oversees 145 island campsites, 46 day-use sites, 42 cruiser campsites and 25 mainland campsites.

Camping permits are issued either on a first-come, first-served basis or by reservation. Every campsite now has a boat dock, picnic table, privy, and a fireplace, and some have a tent platform. Permits issued at the Glen and Narrow Island headquarters are valid for a maximum of two weeks, while those issued at Long Island are valid for three weeks. Campers wishing to stay longer can do so on a day-to-day basis as long as the site is not needed by other campers. The restrictions on the length of stay apply only from July 1 through Labor Day.

The number of campers has varied greatly over the years. In 1962, the state-owned islands hosted 16,904 campers. In 1983, however, the number was 24,977, and in 1995 a total of 22,000 individual campers were registered.

The sites administered by the Glen Island headquarters are the most popular, with the percentage of daily occupancy reaching approximately 95 percent in July and 85 percent in August. The Long Island headquarters generally registers a 65 percent occupancy rate in July. The average stay of a camper on the Lake George islands is currently 3.5 days.

First Aid and Medical
Treatment of Island Users

Throughout the summers when I was on the lake, the number of individuals on the islands on any given day often exceeded 800. These include campers as well as day users. Thus, it is hardly surprising that medical emergencies sometimes arose. It was common practice for anyone who became ill or who suffered an injury to come first to the Glen Island ranger station to seek advice, assistance, or first aid.

Most island users held the campsite rangers in high esteem and undoubtedly thought that the ranger could solve any problem which might come up, including those requiring first aid. Although it was by no means standard DEC policy for ranger stations to be so equipped, at Glen Island we had an "unofficial" first-aid station with sewing needles of all sizes, a few pairs of small scissors, tweezers, petroleum jelly, aspirin, calamine lotion, baking soda, rubbing alcohol, and hydrogen peroxide. We also had a rattlesnake-bite kit which we fortunately never had to use.

The type of first aid we administered during those years is today no longer available at Glen Island. As people have become more and more "sue happy," it would be much too risky to provide this good Samaritan service. However, during all the years we administered our simple first aid we never had a single complaint about any of the treatments.

I enjoyed helping people out, and most especially the children. The problems were usually minor. But, for a child who is suffering, any problem is always a major one. Our assistance often consisted of offering moral support while removing a splinter under a fingernail, or comforting a youngster suffering from a bad case of the homesick blues. Occasionally, our "emergencies" involved a child who was in tears because the camping trip was being spoiled by one rainy day after another.

For the removal of splinters we used needles, scissors, and tweezers which we sterilized by holding over a lit match or by dipping in rubbing alcohol. Many of these under-the-fingernail splinters resulted from sliding a rope up the post on a dock while untying a boat. Youngsters running barefoot along the docks at Glen Island would often get tiny splinters which were easy to remove as long as the youngster could sit still long enough for us to perform the "operation." After swabbing the wound with hydrogen peroxide, we would send the little patients on their merry way.

The children were less appreciative than the parents, but could one blame them? However, I remember one youngster who returned to Glen Island the next day to ask me to be photographed with him. He was very grateful, he said, because I had saved him a trip to the doctor, a fate which he feared more than anything.

Bee stings and insect bites also were common. The honeybee leaves its stinger in the victim and it must be removed in order to prevent infection. A paste of baking soda and water spread on the bee sting or insect bite was generally all the first aid that was required. However, occasionally we encountered a camper with an allergy to bee stings. This can be a dangerous situation requiring professional medical attention. I recall we had to send one doctor to Glens Falls Hospital after he was stung.

For the occasional case when a child camping with a group and perhaps away from home for the first time would come to the island in tears, I found the best medicine to be a little TLC. I would tell the homesick child about the wonders of the lake, the places to go and the things to do. Generally this did the trick and the child left the island with a smile, looking forward to new adventures on the lake.

I recall a couple of these youngsters who returned as campers in later years, stopping by Glen Island to reminisce about their homesickness and their rainy day trials and tribulations. It was this type of incident which made my job as a ranger especially rewarding.

Minor burns (either from the sun or a campfire), poison ivy, and cuts and scrapes were among the other injuries we saw. Severe cuts, where the bleeding could not be stopped, were considered to be medical emergencies requiring a doctor's attention. Also, any foreign body embedded beneath the skin and any sprains and strains were a doctor's call, not ours.

Another frequent injury was the fish hook embedded in the skin. Once a camper asked me to remove such a hook, suggesting that he could supervise the operation since he had once removed one from a fellow fisherman. I politely told him that this operation was beyond my area of expertise. Because it was a windy day and the poor fisherman had only a canoe, I told him that we would transport him by boat to Bolton Landing, where he could pay a visit to the local expert in fish-hook removal, Dr. Leonard Busman. By the next day, the fellow was back out in his canoe fishing, with a large bandage on his left shoulder.

Over the years we were able to ease the pain and fright of many individuals in need of first aid. But a real expression of gratitude is owed to Bolton Landing's Dr. Busman, as well as to Dr. Robert Rosen, a long-time Mohican Island camper, both of whom provided countless services to Lake George island campers.

THE CAMPER
I'LL NEVER FORGET

D URING MY many years of service, I met a wide variety of
individuals. But there was one particular camper who really
stands out in my memory and who I will surely never forget. His
name was Sandy and, as I recall, it was the summer of 1950 that he
first arrived at headquarters on Glen Island, having hitched a ride
from Bolton Landing. He didn't want to spend the money to rent a
canoe or boat, but he had made up his mind that he was going to
camp on an island.

Upon his arrival, Sandy told me his predicament. He explained that
he wanted to be assigned a campsite as close as possible to the
headquarters so that he could easily get back and forth to the
commissary. I gave him site 4 on Phantom Island, located about 50
feet from Glen.

Every morning, Sandy would swim the short distance across to
Glen Island to get his groceries. Being a good swimmer, he managed
to get his provisions back to his campsite without even getting them
wet. He kept them high and dry by holding them above his head as he
propelled himself through the water by kicking his feet. It was quite a
hilarious sight to see his head bobbing in the water, hands in the air, as
he made his way back to Phantom.

Sandy stayed on Phantom for about four weeks, socializing with
other campers by hitching boat rides from island to island. As word
spread of his hilarious daily excursions between Phantom and Glen, a
crowd often gathered to watch as he made his way home with a loaf of
bread and a bottle of milk clutched above his head.

The other campers admired Sandy for his ingenuity and
persistence. We all missed him when he did not return in subsequent

years. For several summers thereafter we reminisced about him fondly, hoping that he would suddenly show up to entertain us with his antics. But we never saw him again. Sandy, if you read this, even if you are old and gray, please come back to Lake George for a visit. We miss you; we need your humor. And I promise that if you come back I will personally arrange for a boat ride to get you out to the islands.

DOCTORS BUSMAN & ROSEN

Two DOCTORS—one practicing in Bolton for over half a century and one an inveterate Lake George island camper—have played an important role in my life and in the lives of many campers.

During his 50 years as a doctor, Dr. Leonard Busman of Bolton Landing was often called upon by visitors to the islands. It seems that campers, particularly the inexperienced ones, are prone to injuries and accidents, and Dr. Busman was always available to respond to their calls for help.

Doc Busman could probably write an entire book about his experiences with campers. The maladies he treated included rattlesnake and dog bites, broken bones, knife and ax wounds, bee stings, burns, splinters, ear infections, and last, but not least, embedded fish hooks.

Doc became somewhat of an expert in the removal of fish hooks from all parts of the body. First he gave the patient a shot of novocaine to deaden the pain. He then pushed the hook through the skin until the barb protruded, cut off the barb or shank close to the skin, and drew the unbarbed portion gently through the skin. Finally, he cleaned and dressed the wound. His surgical tool for this operation was a pair of side-cutting pliers purchased at Ron's Hardware Store in Bolton Landing.

Throughout my many years on the lake, we took countless patients to Doc Busman's mainland office. Most of the trips were of an emergency nature. Many of the injuries or illnesses could be handled in his practice, but some of the patients had to be taken to the hospital for further treatment.

In his authority as Warren County Coroner, Dr. Busman was often called upon to investigate deaths. One incident worthy of mention was the drowning of two youths—aged 12 and 15—in late August 1957. Doc Busman and I, along with members of the Boston Rescue Squad (Ken Palmer, Robert Smith, Arthur French, and Ross French), worked on both boys for over an hour in the pouring rain. It was, however, to no avail. Doc Busman did not want to give up his resuscitation efforts, but Dr. Blodgett of Chestertown, also a Warren County Coroner, pronounced both boys dead.

Once, Doc Busman had the opportunity to offer medical assistance to a fellow doctor—Dr. Robert Rosen of Mountain Lakes, New Jersey. Dr. Rosen and his family have been camping on the Lake George islands for over 40 years. His wife's parents camped on the islands 60 years ago.

My relationship with Dr. Rosen began on his first trip to the islands when he introduced himself to me and said he was available for any emergencies that might occur. During the many years that followed, I took him up on his offer many times and he was able to help a great number of campers.

In 1962 an odd incident occurred when a group of Boy Scouts from Camp Chingachgook in Pilot Knob was camping on the shore near Black Mountain. One of the counselors came to Glen Island with a very sick boy who was complaining of sharp pains in the lower right part of his abdomen. The counselor thought it might be an attack of appendicitis. I knew that Doc Rosen was camping on Mohican Island, and I loaded the boy and his counselor into the state boat, the *Banshee*, and headed to the Rosens' campsite.

Doc met us at the shoreline and climbed into the boat to examine the camper. After poking around the painful area and asking several questions, the doctor said he had good news for everyone. "It's not appendicitis," he proclaimed, "just a tummy ache or a touch of intestinal flu."

The good news for the patient, however, was followed by some bad luck for the doctor. As he leaped from the boat back onto the shore in the dark, he landed on a sharp rock, twisting his ankle. We heard him wince in pain. The poor doctor had no choice but to treat himself, taking several pain killers to help him make it through the night. The next morning he went to Dr. Busman's office to have his injury X-rayed and discovered that he had a fracture in his ankle. After a trip to Glen Falls Hospital to have a cast put on his ankle, Doc Rosen returned to his Mohican Island campsite, hobbling about on crutches for the remainder of his vacation. To this day, he and his family still come to Lake George every summer and still camp on their favorite site on Mohican Island.

I will never forget Dr. Rosen's dedication to his profession and his wonderful bedside manner. Many times over the years I have consulted him about medical problems and have always been very grateful for his sage and sound advice.

But it is not just for medical advice that I have relied on Dr. Rosen. He was instrumental in my decision to write this book and has been a great inspiration every step of the way.

OUTHOUSE STORIES

ONE OF LIFE'S modern comforts that nobody wants to have to do without—whether at home or away, whether in a four-star urban hotel or at a remote island campsite—is the toilet. In my conversations with campers over a span of 42 years, I have heard the island toilets referred to by a multitude of names—restrooms, johns, larries, latrines, the head, outhouses, backhouses, chick-sales, s—-houses, pit privies, and port-a-johns. But no matter what they might be called, these facilities are the source of countless memories and many a good laugh, too.

Now, I'm sure that there is not a person among you who does not know what the primary purpose of the outhouse is. Don't think for a minute, however, that campers always have restricted themselves solely to that use. I am truly amazed at the number of different uses which campers—using good old American ingenuity—have been able to find for this structure. It often serves as a storage shed for extra camping gear. It becomes a sanctuary for many an embattled parent wishing to escape the chaos of rambunctious children, or for a child hoping, perhaps, to avoid camp chores. The outhouse can serve as a quiet reading room—though the lighting leaves a lot to be desired—as well as a shelter for campers arriving in the midst of a storm. I've seen campers turn it into a woodshed, a place where their firewood is sure to stay dry, come rain or high water. Once, in the days before pets were prohibited on state-owned islands, I even saw a dog leashed to a nearby tree and the outhouse door left open so that the dog could take refuge in the event of rain.

Many campers take great pleasure in keeping the interior of their outhouse clean and attractive. Some install oilcloth, while others even hang pictures or a mirror to make it more homey.

Big Burnt and Uncas have long been favorite camping islands for families. Far away from any televisions, videos, or computer games, the children turn toward other forms of entertainment. A favorite game throughout the years, particularly at dusk, has always been hide and seek. And, of course, the outhouse has always served as a hiding place, often being the last place that seekers would want to look. It is easy to imagine that, on at least a few occasions, it became such a good hiding place that the hider surrendered voluntarily rather than having to spend one more minute in this somewhat less-than-aromatic refuge. Some teenagers have used the outhouse as a target for knife throwing, while for others it has served as a dart board.

Vandalism occurred periodically on the islands, usually during the off season. Here, too, a new use for the outhouse was found, as doors and roofs were torn off to be used as firewood.

I sometimes came across an outhouse that had been tipped over and left lying on its side. I must admit that I cannot recall witnessing a single incident of an outhouse being pushed over with someone inside, though I have heard tales of this happening to some unfortunate souls.

I recall vividly a group of campers from New Jersey who returned to the Lake George islands repeatedly between 1959 and 1983. Their primary goal, it seems, was to raise a little Cain and have fun doing it. After my retirement in 1983, this group, which referred to itself as the Troops, admitted to me that a favorite prank had been to ignite cherry bombs and throw them into the hole of the outhouse seat. Today, some of the Troops still come to the lake, and one or two of the families have bought property here. I have no doubt that any of these individuals who chances to read this book will recognize himself immediately as one of the pranksters. It was a fun group of people who occasionally went somewhat overboard in the pursuit of happiness. To their credit, I must add that this same fun-loving group could rise to the occasion when there was serious work to be done, as they so dramatically proved when they assisted us in extinguishing a forest fire on Sagamore Island in the late 1950s.

185

There was a time, back in the 1950s, when campers on some of the larger islands, such as Big Burnt and Turtle, had to share outhouses with other campsites. Although the vast majority were good campers who kept the outhouses neat and clean, there were always a few miscreants who did not share this sense of responsibility. Some campers thus disliked sharing the outhouse with neighboring campsites and would bring along a "Port-a-john" camping toilet which gave them sole and exclusive rights to their own facility. The disadvantage was that these toilets were set up in the great outdoors, placing the campers at the mercy of Mother Nature. And, of course, their privacy was *always* at risk during daylight hours.

Some people will go to even greater lengths to avoid having to share an outhouse with a neighbor. Once, while I was patrolling the main channel between Fork and Little Harbor Islands, I spotted two men towing an object which I at first thought was part of a dock or a wooden platform. However, as I drew closer to their boat, I could not believe my eyes. They were, in fact, towing an outhouse across the channel to their Fork Island campsite. Upon questioning, they revealed that they were bringing it to their campsite in order to have their own private facility. I told them that they would have to take the outhouse back to Little Harbor Island and re-install it. As you can well imagine, the two were a sheepish pair indeed as they turned their boat and cargo around and headed back to Little Harbor.

Prior to 1955, it was the campers' responsibility to burn or bury their tin cans, bottles, and garbage. The outhouse became a favorite disposal site and it was not uncommon to find these items, along with razor blades, cigarette butts, and other trash on the ground when we had to move the outhouses, which was one of the rangers' responsibilities. I also found various items which children had thrown down the hole, including comic books, crayons, pencils, and toys. A fellow ranger once found a man's wallet in the outhouse pit. In later years, disposable diapers became a problem.

It is not only during the regular camping season that outhouses have served other purposes. The ice fishermen on Lake George own shanties which they push out onto the ice, enabling them to fish in warmth and comfort on cold winter days. Some of these ice fishermen once told me the tale of their encounter with a couple of fellow fishermen who were looking for a shanty to use. Setting off for the nearest island, the two found an outhouse and dragged it out onto the ice. The ideal shanty, they must have thought to themselves, already equipped with a seat as well as a hole to fish through. However, these would-be fishermen were thwarted in their adventure when the legitimate ice-shanty owners, upon recognizing the structure as an outhouse, directed them in no uncertain terms to return it to the island forthwith.

It is my hope that you have enjoyed reading these tales as much as I have enjoyed reminiscing about them. And perhaps a reader or two among you will recall with a smile—and a sigh of relief at not being mentioned by name—your own involvement in one of the above-mentioned exploits!

(Above) Betty Leonbruno and Malvina with the fawns.

(Right) Camper bottle-feeding a fawn.

(Below) Betty Leonbruno feeding the fawns.

All photos by Frank Leonbruno, 1972.

188

The Fawns

THROUGHOUT MY many years on the lake, I had many memorable experiences, some funny, some happy, some sad. But the following certainly ranks among the most unusual.

It was Memorial Day weekend of 1972, and a group of Boy Scouts had arrived for a stay on Uncas Island campsite 4. Naturally, one of the first things the boys wanted to do was to explore the island. As they set out to scout the relatively deserted island, they soon discovered two tiny fawns near their campsite.

Their first thought was to "rescue" them, bringing them to safety at the ranger station on Glen Island. The deer were small enough so that the boys could easily carry them, placing them carefully in their boat and making their way to Glen Island.

I remember the arrival of these six scouts, brimming over with excitement as they told me about their discovery. The first question I asked them was if they had seen the mother doe. They told me that they, along with other campers, had searched everywhere but to no avail. Bob Rostetter, ranger at Glen Island, returned to Uncas with the boys to help search once again for the mother. But she was nowhere to be found. Kevin Conerty, operator of the commissary on Glen Island, and I also combed the island. And still no mother deer.

We concluded that a dog on the mainland had driven the pregnant doe into the lake and she then swam to Uncas Island and gave birth to the two fawns. We also decided that the fawns were probably one or two days old and that the doe had fled the island when the Boy Scouts arrived. It was a very unusual case since a doe generally will not abandon her young. Now we were faced with the dilemma of how to care for these two orphans, a job in which we were certainly lacking in experience and training. Fortunately, my wife Betty and Kevin's wife Malvina came to the rescue. Serving as surrogate mothers, they took turns feeding the fawns milk from baby bottles, even staying up at night with them. The fawns readily accepted the bottled milk, sucking eagerly on the nipples.

We all became quite attached to the baby deer, keeping them inside the cabin headquarters in the old post office room and taking turns caring for them. After about a week of nursing from the bottle, our Bambis were ready to eat soft food.

News of the fawns spread quickly among the island campers and many stopped by to see and photograph them. Kevin and I built an outdoor pen where the two deer had room to run about and where campers could feed them.

The fawns grew quickly and, by about six weeks of age, had become very frisky. One of them in particular enjoyed kicking anyone who came too close. Finally, my supervisor at DEC, Russ Mulvey, told us that we could no longer keep them on the island and that we would have to release them.

We all felt that they would not be able to survive on their own in the wilderness. Russ agreed and set about trying to find a home for them. He located a woman who had a small game preserve in the Adirondacks who was willing to adopt our now-famous fawns.

On the day of the fawns' departure from Glen Island, a number of camping families came to say goodbye. Many of the children had tears in their eyes as they watched the two Bambis they had grown to love being taken off the island. They couldn't bear the thought of them going into the wilds of the Adirondacks. But we assured them that they were being taken to a good home, one which would be far more suitable for them than an island on Lake George.

I am certain that many of the children who came to visit these adorable fawns on Glen Island returned home with wonderful tales for their friends and teachers about the deer they got to know while camping on Lake George.

Dogs on the Islands

I N THE EARLY years of camping on Lake George, the presence of dogs on state-owned islands was never a problem. In those days, there were far fewer campers. And because many of the campers occupied their island sites for the entire summer it would have been unthinkable for them not to bring their pets along.

After World War II, as island camping became increasingly popular, the state saw the need to limit the amount of time that campers could remain on an island site. Throughout the 1950s and '60s, the stay was restricted to six weeks. It was later decreased to four weeks and, in 1994, the DEC limited the stay to a maximum of two weeks. Over the years, the number of dogs on the islands increased continuously, as did the problems connected with these pets.

Between 1957 and 1977 various attempts were made to ban dogs from all state campgrounds. Committees consisting of DEC supervisory personnel, responsible for camping areas across the state, were formed to study the problem. The committees invariably recommended that dogs be prohibited. There was already a state regulation requiring that dogs be on a leash at all campsites. However, while this was easy to enforce at mainland campgrounds, it was nearly impossible to ensure that dogs on islands were leashed.

As a result, the dogs continued to roam free on the islands. They frolicked in the lake (also illegal) and deposited their excrement all over the islands, creating a mess as well as offensive odors. Furthermore, there were numerous cases where our employees as well as campers were attacked and bitten by dogs. I was among those having this unfortunate experience. Many was the time that we had to consult Dr. Busman, health officer for the town of Bolton, about the

191

need for quarantining a dog which had bitten someone and which had no proof of a recent rabies vaccination.

But often it was the dogs themselves who suffered on a camping trip. Dog fights broke out occasionally, one time even resulting in the death of one of the combatants. Occasionally a dog, leashed to a dock post by its owner, drowned after jumping or falling into the water. Because of the short leash or difficult terrain, the dog was unable to climb back onto the dock or onto shore and met a disastrous fate. The campers involved in these tragic incidents intended no harm to their pets, but were simply unaware of the dangers.During the summer of 1967 alone three dogs drowned in the lake.

Many dogs were lost and had to be kept at headquarters until the owners could be located. In a few cases, the owners could not be located, and I recall one or two camping parties who adopted the dogs when the owners were not found. One ranger boarded a lost dog for two weeks, and I looked after another one for a week. Another DEC employee actually adopted a dog permanently after the owners could not be traced.

Another problem with unleashed dogs was their attraction to the waters of Lake George. Campers who were not dog owners and not dog fanciers complained bitterly about dogs swimming in their drinking water.

Campers who had come to Lake George to enjoy its peace and serenity also complained about barking dogs at neighboring sites. Sometimes dogs would tree a raccoon, running around the trunk and barking endlessly at the frightened wildlife.

One year the garbage crew boycotted a particular campsite on Perch Island. The dog on that site would not allow the crew to collect the garbage. In fact, the dog attacked and bit them whenever they came near. To resolve this problem, the owner of the dog put his garbage in his own boat and transported it to the garbage scow which waited about 200 feet offshore.

I remember a couple who left a dog unattended on Gem Island for almost five days without enough food or water. A camper from Big Burnt Island reported the incident to us and, upon the couple's return, we immediately canceled their camping permit. Fortunately, the camper from Big Burnt took it upon himself to supply the poor mutt with food and water until the owners' return.

One day I saw a dog swimming in the open waters of the lake between Fourteen Mile Island and Dome. I recognized the dog immediately as belonging to Dick and Claire Bartlett, owners of a summer home on Fourteen Mile Island. The Bartletts had gone by boat to the Lake George Club. Their dog Rufus apparently had so much affection for his owners that he wanted to be with them even if it meant swimming the 4.5 miles to the club. All's well that ends well, and Rufus was rescued from the lake and returned to his owners.

In 1970, brown dog ticks and American dog ticks were discovered on Duran Island. The ticks had been carried to the island by dogs from Long Island. The New York State Museum and Science Service of the Department of Education confirmed the fact that the infestation could have a potentially serious impact on island camping on Lake George. Known to carry Rocky Mountain spotted fever, the ticks presented a danger to campers.

At that point, the Department of Education strongly recommended that dogs be banned from the islands. DEC declined to issue such a regulation, but did authorize the spraying of carbaryl to eradicate the ticks from Duran. It also prohibited camping on that island for the duration of that summer. Surveys conducted in the fall of 1971 showed that the ticks had been eradicated from Duran. Dogs continued to be allowed on the islands.

In 1974, DEC hired two park rangers whose sole responsibility was to bring the dog problem under control. These two men issued about 400 warnings to owners of non-leashed dogs. They also kept statistics on the numbers of dogs on the islands, establishing that one out of every four camping parties was accompanied by a dog. Many of these parties had two or more dogs, with one group even bringing along five.

In 1975, ticks were reported on Fork and Big Burnt islands. However, no large infestations developed either that year or in subsequent seasons. In July 1975, Director Hugo Jamnback of the State Museum and Science Service recommended strongly that dogs be prohibited on state-owned islands. But it was not until March 24, 1977, that DEC Commissioner Peter Berle finally demonstrated the courage which other commissioners had not. He promulgated rules and regulations banning dogs from all state-owned islands on Lake George.

I could not close this chapter on dogs without stating that I am well aware of the affection that many campers have for their pets. I fully realize how much a part of a family a pet becomes. However, we must also recognize that man's best friend (his dog) could become a nightmare for a neighboring camper, as evidenced by the above tales.

I spent 38 camping seasons on Glen Island. During that time my wife and I owned three dogs, each of whom we adored. When the ban on dogs was issued in 1977, I personally took a lot of heat from campers who for years had been bringing their dogs along on their annual camping trips and who were outraged by the new regulations. I feel, however, that the careful evaluation of the problems associated with pets on Lake George justified the actions taken. The prohibition is in the best interest of all of the thousands of campers who visit the beautiful islands of Lake George each year.

Tales of
Mohican Island Cats

O N Labor Day weekend of 1956, a family which had been
camping on Mohican Island came to Glen Island to report that
they needed to return immediately to their home in New Jersey due
to an emergency. However, they told me, their cat was still on the
island. He had run away each time they tried to catch him.

The family gave me their home address and telephone number in
the hope that another camper would retrieve the cat and bring it to
Glen Island. The cat, they said, was black with a red collar around its
neck.

Campers came and left throughout the remainder of the summer.
All reported the same cat with a red collar, a cat who was not at all
cooperative in attempts to capture it. When autumn came and I
realized that the cat must still be on Mohican Island, I grew somewhat
concerned.

Throughout September, my crew and I placed food at campsite 6
on Mohican. And each time we returned, the food had been devoured.
The cat was spotted repeatedly, but whenever we tried to catch him he
ran away.

The days grew cold in October, and still the cat evaded us.
November arrived and it was time to pull the state boat, the *Banshee*,
out of the water for the winter. My crew and I discussed the fate of the
cat and decided we had to put him out of his misery. There was no
way he could survive the winter. The next day we brought along our
guns and headed for the island. Deer hunting was still legal, and we
decided that if we didn't get the cat then we might at least get a deer.

As Ranger Wyman Russell and I approached campsite 6 in the
boat, Wyman yelled, "Frank, look! There's a bobcat."

I couldn't believe my eyes, but sure enough, there stood a bobcat, clear as day. And no sign of our red-collared black house cat. The bobcat ran to the south end of the island. We climbed out of the boat, hugging the shoreline as we followed the wild animal. The island is very narrow, and we could see across its entire width. As I approached the west shoreline, I suddenly saw the bobcat coming toward me. I stopped in my tracks. The bobcat came within 20 feet of me and also stopped. I had little choice but to point my gun and shoot. It was an easy target and one shot brought him down.

We never did see the black cat or find any of its remains. Some imaginative souls might argue that the cat had grown so wild that it had turned into a bobcat. But, being of a more realistic bent, I believe that the poor black cat had been howling at night, attracting the bobcat from the nearby shore. The bobcat had been rewarded for his curiosity and his icy swim with an easy prey. As for Wyman and myself, we were rewarded with a $25 check from Warren County, which at that time was the bounty placed on bobcats.

RATTLESNAKES
ON LAKE GEORGE

RATTLESNAKES HAVE been present in the Tongue Mountain area for hundreds, if not thousands, of years. The type found here, known as the timber rattlesnake (*Crotalus horridus*), is the only deciduous forest rattlesnake widely found in the eastern United States. Rattlesnake dens have been found in Warren, Washington, and Essex Counties, as well as in Clinton and Saratoga Counties.

The wooded and rocky terrain of the Tongue Mountain Range provides a natural habitat for rattlers. During July and August, rattlesnakes have been known to swim from the shoreline out to some of the islands. Rattlers have been spotted on Steere, Hatchet, East Dollar, West Dollar, Halfway, Turtle, Juanita, Sarah, Hazel, and Duran Islands.

During my 42 years of service with the DEC, my colleagues and I killed about 15 rattlesnakes. We never actually went looking for the snakes, but rather were called into service by campers, day users, and even boaters who spotted the rattlers. The first rattlesnake I encountered was on Duran Island, back in 1945. This snake had crawled under an abandoned tent platform and, despite our prodding with sticks and boat paddles, refused to come out in the open. We decided that the best course of action would be to set the platform on fire in order to coax the snake out. This did the trick. When the snake emerged, a camper hit it with a paddle, killing it instantly.

On August 21, 1959, I killed a 4.5-foot rattler on Sarah Island. This large snake, bearing 13 rattles, was spotted by Tink Shaw, a pilot of the cruise boat *Roamer*. He followed its course through the water until it wriggled its way up onto the island. He then steered his vessel to

Glen Island to report the sighting to me. I went immediately to Sarah Island, where I found the snake after a short search.

Another rattler worthy of note was reported by campers on East Dollar Island. The campers were eating their breakfast when they noticed a rattlesnake at their picnic table. Although they did not realize the danger which the snake presented, they came to Glen Island to apprise us of the situation. We accompanied the campers back to the island where we found the rattler coiled around a cross-brace under the picnic table.

During my years on Lake George there were no deaths caused by rattlesnake bites. Furthermore, to the best of my knowledge, no island camper on Lake George has ever been bitten by a rattlesnake. I do, however, recall one incident where a hiker on Tongue Mountain was bitten by a rattlesnake and had to be transported to the Glens Falls Hospital by the Bolton Rescue Squad. It seems that the hiker wandered off the trail, tripped, and fell on top of the snake, which then bit him on the wrist. The injury, however, was not serious, and the hiker was treated and discharged the same day.

My narration regarding rattlesnakes on Lake George would not be complete without mentioning Dr. William S. Brown, professor of biology at Skidmore College and a leading authority on Adirondack rattlesnakes. He has been studying the life cycles, hibernation patterns, and reproductive biology of these reptiles since the late 1970s. Dr. Brown has discovered that females reach maturity at an average age of 10 years. They bear an average of nine young every three to four years thereafter. He has also found that the rattler is a homebody, rarely straying more than a mile or two from its den. In 1983, Dr. Brown was instrumental in getting the rattlesnake placed on the state's list of endangered and threatened species.

In earlier years, many rattlers fell prey to bounty hunters who were rewarded with a $5 payment for each rattle presented. This practice was discontinued in 1971 to the great joy of many town clerks, who had acted as the depository for the rattles. I remember that the rattles presented to the town clerks needed to have at least two inches of the tail attached. Before this requirement was adopted, bounty hunters would simply remove the rattles, release the rattlesnake and recapture it at a later time.

In the days before the bounty was outlawed, a rattlesnake hunter named Willie Clark lived north of Bolton Landing. He stalked the slopes of Tongue Mountain and knew the snake dens by names, such as Pine Tree Den. It is said that he produced snake oil, marketing it as a cure for rheumatism. Many old-timers also claim that the snake oil worked wonders in curing earaches.

In 1983, in cooperation with DEC employees on Glen Island, Dr. Brown embarked on a program to capture any "nuisance" rattlers reported on the state camping islands. Since that time, rangers are trained in the use of snake tongs with which they can safely capture a snake and place it in a container. The rangers then contact Dr. Brown, who returns the snake to its home in the mountains. Prior to releasing the snake, however, Dr. Brown marks it for identification purposes.

Dr. Brown and the rangers have become very familiar with one particular rattler which was first captured in 1984. By 1990, in fact, he had gotten to know this snake so well that he named it Champ. From 1990 to 1995, Champ was captured each year—and sometimes even several times within one year—on his favorite island, Turtle Island. Champ's recovery, and that of a handful of similar rattlers each year, demonstrates a successful public-private cooperative program, a program which protects the public and at the same time protects a threatened wildlife species.

Before closing this chapter, I would like to issue a word of warning. Anyone spotting a rattlesnake should not try to capture it. Rather, he or she should report its presence to the ranger station at Glen Island. Not only are these rangers trained in the capture of the snakes, but they are also properly equipped. Although a rattlesnake will generally not attack humans unless provoked, it is a pretty safe bet that the snake would view any attempt to capture it as a provocation.

WHO IS THIS MASKED
ROBBER OF THE ISLANDS?

A NY TALES about island wildlife would not be complete without a chapter about the raccoon, also known as the masked robber, ringtail, or Mr. Monkey Mitts. The latter nickname derives from the fact that the raccoon's front feet are as dexterous as a monkey's hands. It is the rare camper on Lake George who has not been visited by a raccoon at some point during an island stay. This extraordinary animal, whose facial markings resemble a mask, is referred to by many—somewhat less than affectionately—as the Island Thief. Generally campers are forewarned by campsite rangers about the raccoons and provided with tips on how to deal with this sly and cunning critter.

The raccoon uses his 10 long, soft-skinned fingers and 10 toes with great skill in accomplishing his mission—scavenging for food. Mr. Ringtail has no difficulty in prying the top off a garbage can. He can even undo simple knots or remove stones which campers often place on top of a food box to protect its contents. Because raccoons are excellent swimmers, they have no problem getting to the islands from the mainland. They have a keen sense of smell and are anything but fussy about their diet. They will eat birds and their eggs, crayfish, frogs, fish, and any fruit or vegetable. But among their favorite treats are the groceries and garbage of the campers.

During the camping season, raccoons are found on almost all of the Lake George islands. Turtle Island, with its 33 campsites and its proximity to an expanse of largely undeveloped mainland, always has been a popular habitat. Long Island, with its 100 acres and 90 campsites, is another choice location for raccoons.

Since most campers store an assortment of delectable victuals at their campsites, raccoons truly have a wide range of menu choices during the summer months. These thieves will take advantage of any opportunity to raid food supplies. How many campers have climbed out of their sleeping bags early in the morning with visions of bacon and eggs dancing in their heads only to discover that the Masked Robber had already enjoyed this very breakfast? How many hot-dog roasts, intended as a treat for the kiddies, had to be canceled when the parents discovered that the main course had been devoured by a raccoon? And how many steaks have ended up in the stomach of the Island Thief rather than sizzling on the grill simply because someone forgot to secure the cover of the cooler?

I had a surprise encounter with a raccoon one spring when I went out to Glen Island shortly after ice-out to start opening up the headquarters for the season. Since the weather was still nippy, my first task was to light a fire in the living quarters. However, before loading the wood in the fireplace, I opened the chimney damper to create a draft. Imagine my shock when suddenly a raccoon fell down onto the hearth with a thud. The poor creature had probably trapped himself in the chimney in the autumn, unable to move up or down, and had starved to death. I was glad to have discovered him before I lit the fire, though some acquaintances swear that roast raccoon is a real delicacy.

Excellent climbers, despite a weight of up to 20 pounds, raccoons spend their days hiding in branches of trees. It is at night that they become active, prowling about in search of food to be stolen from the unsuspecting camper. And not only do these uninvited dinner guests eat the camper out of house and home, but they are also so rude as to make no effort whatsoever to clean up after themselves. Insult is added to injury as campers often awaken to the unwelcome sight of trash cans tipped over on their sides and the contents strewn across the campsite. In the days when trash was still picked up from the islands by the state garbage crew, the crew also often found this same scenario as they made their morning rounds. It was not uncommon to find a dead raccoon among the garbage on the islands. Obviously some campers—or even some DEC employees—retaliated against this pest by putting him to sleep forever. This was, of course, illegal.

Raccoons are protected outside of hunting season (mid-October through mid-February) and stiff fines are imposed upon anyone violating this law. Only in cases where a raccoon is found to be rabid can a law enforcement official kill the animal.

It is not just during the night hours that problems occur with raccoons. During the era prior to the prohibition of dogs on islands (dogs were banned in 1977), it was not uncommon for a dog to tree a raccoon. One can easily imagine the commotion caused by such an incident. Just picture one or more dogs barking most of the day and night at a treed animal. We were frequently called to the scene, in which case we generally persuaded the dog's owner to either remove the pet from the island temporarily or at least take him to another campsite until the raccoon could escape.

A raccoon once bit a sleeping camper on Turtle Island. Although raccoons generally prefer to gnaw, their teeth are sharp enough to inflict a potentially serious bite. When this particular camper came to Glen Island to report his injury, which turned out to be little more than a scratch, I decided to play it safe and send him to Doc Busman in Bolton Landing. Although the doctor was initially concerned about the possibility of rabies, the fear fortunately proved to be unfounded in this case.

To alleviate the problem during my tenure, we captured as many raccoons as possible, using a cage live trap baited with bacon grease. We then transported the trapped animals to the mainland near the foot of Tongue Mountain, releasing them in this uninhabited, wooded terrain. One DEC employee told me that he personally trapped and relocated 66 raccoons during a recent camping season (1994).

Although raccoons were definitely a nuisance, these intelligent animals also often delighted many of the island campers, particularly the children. Before the recent spread of rabies, it was not uncommon for campers to feed raccoons from their hands. However, officials today strongly warn against any contact with raccoons. In fact, they highly recommend that, when picking up garbage strewn by these animals, gloves be worn as an added protection against rabies infection.

THE LAKE GEORGE
QUILL PIG

THE PORCUPINE has been called by many names—porky, woods pig, quill pig, bristle pig, wasteful whittler, walking pincushion, as well as a few names which I would not want to put in print. The following description of this pesky critter will do much to explain how these names developed.

The porcupine is a rather unattractive animal, clumsy and slow as molasses in his movements. Taking short steps, he waddles from side to side as he walks. When ambling through the woods, he sounds like the rustle of leaves. In the Adirondacks, his diet consists of leaves, bark, grasses, herbs, and, where available, water lilies and other aquatic plants.

With his four long, sharp incisors, the porcupine is classified as a rodent, albeit without the intelligence exhibited by other rodents. The porcupine has sharp-curved claws and padded feet which aid him in climbing trees. Once he goes up in a tree, he will remain there for a considerable length of time, gnawing on the inner bark and tender twigs. On the shoreline near Black Mountain, the porcupine is particularly fond of feeding on elm buds and sugar maple bark during the spring months. In the winter, he will gnaw the bark off hardwood, often totally stripping the trees at their base and causing them to die.

Individuals vacationing on Lake George should be aware that many areas are inhabited by not-so-friendly porcupines. Commission Point, Red Rock Point, and the Black Mountain area are especially common haunts for these critters. The outhouses here have always been a popular destination for the gnawing porcupines. Every year we would make the necessary repairs to these structures by replacing the seats and flooring. In more recent years, fiberglass toilet seats have been installed to discourage these animals. Because the porcupine has a passion for anything which is salt impregnated, he is particularly attracted to ax handles or canoe paddles coated with sweat from human hands.

When attacked by an enemy, the porcupine makes noises, lowers its head and raises the quills on its back and tail. It swats the enemy with its tail, moving this appendage at a remarkably rapid rate and embedding the quills in the enemy's face. These barbed quills are among the cruelest of nature's defense mechanisms. Once anchored in the enemy, they are extremely difficult to remove. Dogs often have tangled with porcupines along the shores of Lake George, with the dog generally drawing the short straw. In such a case, the quills must be removed promptly. Unless the dog's owner is experienced in such removal, it is advisable to seek out the services of a veterinarian. Using pliers or tweezers, the quills are removed by pulling straight out with a quick jerk. Of course, the entire procedure is very painful for the poor hound, but it is a necessary evil.

I cannot recall ever having seen a porcupine on an island or in the lake. However, I do know that this animal can and does swim when threatened by an enemy.

The porcupine was a source of food for early American settlers. In more recent times, hikers and campers were instructed that if they became lost in the woods the porcupine was the only animal which they could easily catch as a food source. However, it is extremely doubtful that today's hikers and campers would find it necessary to hunt down, kill, and eat poor porky. This animal, however much of a pest he is, is part of our environment and is entitled to his place in it. Nevertheless, I am certain that DEC employees would be very pleased if he would just leave the shoreline outhouses out of his diet.

THE RETURN OF THE FROGS

As I LOOK back over my many years on the lake, I recall several incidents which still bring a smile to my face. One of my favorites is the story of the frogs.

My long-time friend Harold Tucker, who now owns a home on Fourteen Mile Island, camped for 50 years, staying on many different islands. In the summer of 1960 he was assigned a site on Uncas Island, just a stone's throw from Glen Island. One day he came over to Glen Island to inquire about the presence of frogs at a spot just west of the Glen Island docks, an area particularly abundant in lily pads. Harold told me that the croaking frogs brought back pleasant memories of his boyhood days in Bayonne, New Jersey, when he was lulled to sleep by their songs. Howard asked whether I would mind if he took three or four frogs from Glen Island back to his campsite, which incidentally had an ideal bay for frogs.

"Help yourself," I told him, adding that the frogs would probably quickly return to their Glen Island lily pads. Thrilled, Harold caught three frogs of substantial size and took them back to his campsite. Much to his dismay, however, there was no croaking of frogs the first night. And none the second night. On the third day, Harold returned to Glen Island and we walked over to the lily pads. I pointed to three large frogs.

"There are your frogs," I told Harold. "They've returned to their home." Now, to be perfectly honest, I did not really believe that these were the same frogs which Harold had taken to Uncas. But I convinced Harold.

He captured the three large frogs and took them over to Gem Island, which is about 1,000 feet from Glen. Over the next couple of days we made several observational field trips to the lily pads. We saw two or three small frogs each time, but no sign of the large ones. On the fifth day, however, we spotted the three big frogs again. Curious about whether or not these were the same frogs, Harold came up with an idea.

"Let's tie a small colored rubber band around one of their hind legs and take them over to Glen again," he suggested. Believe it or not, the three rubber-banded frogs showed up once again at their Glen Island home about four days later.

Several campers from neighboring Uncas and Phantom Islands followed our biology experiment with interest, developing a curiosity about the frogs and their habits. Although I had no scientific explanation for their behavior, I thought to myself that perhaps these frogs had grown as attached to Glen Island as I had. I have since done some reading on frogs and learned that the males stake out their territory by distinctive croaks. These croaks, which serve as the mating call, are recognized by the females of that species. Thus, these frogs simply needed to come back "home"—to their own territory— where their mates would be waiting for them.

One added note: While most of us think of the mating (and thus croaking) season for frogs as being in the spring, the mating season on Lake George is somewhat later owing to the late ice-out on the lake.

SNIPE HUNTING
ON LAKE GEORGE

D URING THE LATTER part of the first half of this century, before
the state stopped issuing seasonal camping permits, families
would camp for the entire summer on a favorite island. These
campers, particularly the youngsters, had plenty of time on their
hands to come up with creative ideas for occupying themselves during
those long summer days. They held swimming contests and treasure
hunts from Glen Island. The older children would come to Glen
Island to await the arrival of the mail boat each day. This gave them
the opportunity to check out dating prospects or to find new friends
among the other campers who were doing exactly the same thing.

Many of these campers also took it upon themselves to break in the
greenhorn campers by taking them on a snipe hunt. In this rite of
initiation, the experienced old-timers told the new campers that the
islands were inhabited by a small flightless bird, the snipe, which made
for a tasty meal if caught. They explained that snipe come out of their
nests only at night and could be lured into a burlap bag by means of a
flashlight.

As night fell, the group would paddle to one of the more remote
uninhabited islands to start the hunt. A small unnamed island near
Commission Island was a particular favorite with the snipe hunters.
After situating the novice at one end of the island and instructing him
or her to sit very still with the burlap bag and flashlight, the rest of the
group would go to the other end of the island to start driving the snipe
toward the bag. Of course, it was at that end of the island that the
canoes happened to be beached. The pranksters would paddle quietly
away, leaving the poor unsuspecting greenhorn to wait in vain for the
snipe. Hours later, the group would return to pick up the person who

had been left holding the bag. By this time, the novice had long since realized that he or she had been the victim of a practical joke.

Pranks like this passed from one generation of camper to the next. Generally, however, there was at least one member of the older generation who considered this ritual barbaric and would warn the novice of the trick. In one instance when this happened, the frustrated "pros" instantly came up with an alternative initiation rite. They snuck up on the novice in the middle of the night, generously dousing him with buckets of water as he slept soundly in his sleeping bag.

Today, one of the instigators is an officer of the 110-year-old Lake George Association, an organization dedicated to protecting the lake. The seeds of his love of and dedication to Lake George were planted during the summers of his youth when he spent many happy weeks in an island tent. He and many of the other young campers would often visit me at Glen Island and we would talk about some of the questionable activities occurring on the lake and how the lake could best be protected. I feel extremely fortunate that I was able to pass my love and concern for the lake on to many of those kids who, in turn, passed it on to their friends and families.

Unfortunately, island camping on Lake George has changed dramatically over the past decades as the pace of life has become more hectic. Today's campers stay only for short periods of time. Many arrive with large modern boats instead of the simple canoes, rowboats, or small outboard craft of years gone by. The personal relationships which developed when all the campers knew their neighbors and learned from each other are also a thing of the past. The feeling of being one big camping family, with everyone returning year after year, is gone. Of course, with the larger turnover, many more people now have the opportunity to experience the lake. But, regrettably, it is a more impersonal experience.

I am sure that the young campers of yesteryear will never forget the good old days of the snipe hunts, the lasting friendships, and those long lazy crazy days of summer. I know that I never will forget these youngsters because they were such an important part of my life and my experience on Lake George.

CANOE SUN BATHING

I REMEMBER receiving a phone call at the Glen Island ranger station in the late 1950s. The caller, a property owner in the Northwest Bay area, was very concerned about two canoeists he had seen paddling from Montcalm Point toward the western shore of Northwest Bay.

It seems that he had his binoculars trained on the young couple in the canoe for several minutes before setting them aside for a few minutes. When he refocused on the canoe there was no sign of the couple. He scanned the entire area, thinking that the pair had perhaps decided to go for a swim. But there were no swimmers to be seen. Only a floating canoe, with no sign of life.

His first thought was that perhaps they had drowned. This, of course, prompted his call to the ranger station. I jumped in the boat and sped toward Northwest Bay. As I rounded Montcalm Point, I saw a red canoe floating peacefully, with no passengers aboard, just as the caller had described.

I drew closer and closer but still could not see any individuals. Finally, when I pulled up alongside the canoe, I got the surprise of my life—as did the young couple lying side-by-side on the floor of the canoe, sun bathing in their birthday suits.

From that point on, I always urged caution in investigating any "abandoned" boats, advising any investigators to make plenty of noise when approaching such a vessel.

THE TALE OF THE SHORT
CUT TO VERMONT

O NE COLD February night in 1969 a stranger stopped at a bar in
Bolton. "What's the shortest route to Vermont?" he asked.
Because Vermont is due east of Lake George, and because Bolton is
on the lake's west shore, the normal route to Vermont would require
driving all the way around the lake. However, this man wanted the
most direct route, and the bartender and his patrons took him at his
word. He could, they told him, drive out onto the ice at the town
dock, just south of Veteran's Park. From there, he should drive north,
turning right at the end of Green Island and head east to Fourteen
Mile Island. Beyond that, they continued, was the Knapp estate,
where he could drive up onto the mainland following a path used by
snowmobilers, fishermen, and the Knapps' caretaker, who traveled
across the ice to Bolton by Jeep. Once on dry land, he would find a
plowed road leading to Fort Ann and on to Vermont.

The stranger headed out onto the lake, following the directions he
had been given. Shortly before reaching Fourteen Mile Island,
however, his first misfortune occurred. Coming upon a pressure ridge
with open water behind it, his vehicle plunged into the icy lake.
Luckily, he was able to escape before the car submerged almost
completely in the shallow water, leaving only the tip of the rear end
above the water.

Soaked to the skin, the young man hiked across the ice to the east
shore, finding refuge in the Knapps' former stable and carriage
house. The building, which had been converted to a storage shed,
housed tools and equipment, as well as a 1968 pick-up truck. Using a
metal barrel and some wood which he found in the building, the
young man built a fire to dry his clothes and keep himself warm.

However, it was at this point that his second misfortune occurred. The barrel proved to be a less than ideal fireplace and, as the fire grew hotter and hotter, the old wooden floor on which it stood caught on fire. It didn't take long before the entire building was engulfed in flames.

The result of a shortcut across Lake George.   *Photo by Walt Grishkot.*

From across the lake, Joe Smith, owner of F. R. Smith and Sons Marina in Bolton, saw the bright orange flames shooting up into the clear night air against the backdrop of the pitch-black mountain. Reaching for the phone, he called Ernest Granger, caretaker for the Knapps. Granger immediately notified the Fort Ann Fire Company before heading to the scene himself. As he sped down Shelving Rock Road from his home in Fort Ann, Granger saw a stranger walking along the road toward him. Suspecting that this man just might have had something to do with the fire, Granger called the New York State Police, who set out to look for the young man. He was not difficult to find, and the police soon had him in custody. Under interrogation, he admitted that he had indeed started the fire, though he explained that he had only done it to warm himself and had no intention of burning the building. Upon learning that he was A.W.O.L. from the U. S. Army, the police turned him over to the military police.

Ralph Stiles (who later succeeded Ernest Granger as caretaker for the Knapp property) and three other volunteers from the Fort Ann Fire Company responded to the fire. Their efforts, however, were in vain. The fire spread quickly, burning the building to the ground. (Stiles, along with Elsa Steinback, who lives adjacent to the Knapp estate, were the source of much of the information contained in this chapter.)

The day after the incident, I took Walt Grishkot, noted photographer of the Lake George region, to the site by snowmobile in order for him to photograph the submerged car.

A trip out onto the ice—be it on foot, skates, cross-country skis, car, snowmobile, or iceboat—can be a thrilling experience. But I would be remiss if I failed to warn you of the dangers of such an exploit. The moods of the lake can be tricky and spots which appear to be solidly frozen may in fact be completely unsafe. Before venturing out onto any frozen surface, I would advise you to be absolutely certain that it can support you.

THE SAGA OF THE LAKE GEORGE TROUT

HISTORICALLY, RECORDS reveal that centuries prior to the arrival of Europeans, the paddle splash of the Native American canoe was not only to enjoy a canoe ride but also to obtain food, namely fish. Most likely, Indians have fished in Lake George for thousands of years. There have been found spear points around beaches that were manufactured in a manner used from 1100 to 1500 years ago. Bones were formed into fish hooks, and netting also was done.

This lake, and the Adirondacks in general, were used only in the summer; the tribes migrated back to the St. Lawrence valley or to the Mohawk River valley for the winter. Only one tribe—the Abenaki—appeared to stay over the winter. This name is said to have meant "bark eaters," reflecting on the meager rations available when the deep snows arrived.

Although there were likely other tribes in the region before them, the earliest tribes were the Algonquins, who were driven north by the Iroquois and their confederates. They used Lake George for the fishing and hunting—when their food dried, they took their catch back to their permanent homes in the Mohawk River valley.

There are areas on Lake George where natural or man-made kettles (roughly two-foot-wide by three-foot-deep basins) were used to steam fish. Rocks were heated in a fire and pushed into the kettles. Fish were put into baskets and suspended in the kettles, water was added, and the kettles were covered. The steam produced cooked the fish and whatever else was added.

Special thanks to John Schaninger, chairman of the LGA Fish and Game Committee, for his technical advice and assistance in writing this chapter.

It appears that the fish inhabiting Lake George prior to the arrival of Europeans included lake trout, brook trout, cisco, whitefish, bullhead, northern pike, emerald shiner, and yellow perch. In the mid- to late-1800s, species such as largemouth and smallmouth bass, landlocked salmon, rainbow trout, sunfish, brown trout, and even walleyed pike were introduced. It is likely that rock bass were also introduced in this time frame. The fish fry or eggs often were brought in by railroad cars; hatcheries were used to further propagate the species. Some of those species, such as the bass and sunfish, took hold and are present in large numbers today. In general, species that reproduced in the lake did well while the stream-spawning species (such as landlocked salmon, brown and rainbow trout) found the relatively short and steep stretches of streams available to them insufficient for adequate spawning. For example, even though there still is a native population of both spring- and fall-spawning rainbow trout, since the stocking was discontinued in the early 1980s fishermen rarely catch them in the lake due to insufficient reproduction.

In the last 25 years, two other species have been introduced as well—the black crappie and the rainbow smelt. These will be discussed later in the chapter.

In the mid- to late-1880s, the grand hotels became very important to the Lake George fisheries. Netters, guides, and locals took lake trout in great numbers, and the trout became a prime source of food at the dinners of the hotels. There were no seasons nor limits on the size or quantity of fish that could be kept, and the populations were decimated to the point where it became hard to catch any trout. At the same time, logging increased runoff and caused heavy siltation and algae blooms, which also damaged reproduction in some areas. Concerned sportsmen formed groups, such as the Lake George Association, as early as 1885 to lobby the state and local governments to protect the fishery and the land. Due in large part to their efforts, laws were enacted. At the same time, the first hatcheries were created, and old records indicate that hundreds of thousands of lake trout were stocked in Lake George as early as the late 1880s by the New York

214

State Conservation Commission, the predecessor of the Department of Environmental Conservation (DEC).

Of all the fish in Lake George, the lake trout traditionally has been the most popular with anglers. Warren County has described it as the "bread and butter" of the fisheries. In the past, the native trout population was supplemented by stocking hatchery fish. Lake George was such a reliable source of lake trout that it was used as a source of eggs and milt for the hatcheries that supplied much of the stocked trout for most of the Adirondacks. This was accomplished by netting wild fish in November, stripping the females of eggs and the males of milt, then transporting the eggs to the hatcheries, where they were grown for one to two years before reintroducing the fry or fingerlings to the various lakes.

In the lake, the lake trout become sexually mature at around six years of age, depending on the available food and the temperature where they live. Spawning occurs from late October to late November over natural rubble at depths from a few feet to 30 feet or so. The most important consideration is that the area must be highly oxygenated and free from silt. (In some lakes, such as Lake Superior, spawning can be at depths exceeding 500 feet.) The trout spawn over rocky areas since the eggs will escape predation in the crevices and will still receive oxygen as the lake water is mixed by waves or current.

In the past, hunters would go out at night in boats with lanterns (or, when they became available, flashlights) to spear lake trout congregated on the rocky spawning beds. Specialized spears, or gigs, were used to take large quantities of spawning trout. Stories have been told of lake trout in excess of 50 pounds being taken this way. With the advent of fishing regulations and seasons, this became against the law.

Following spawning, the eggs lie semi-dormant; they begin to hatch as the water warms up in the spring, typically in April. The young scatter from the spawning area by May, feeding off a sac of nutrients attached to them. When the sac is depleted, the fry will begin to feed on insect eggs, insects, and young opossum shrimp. As the trout grow, the opossum shrimp become their most important food. The opossum shrimp live in large numbers in the sediments at almost all the depths

215

of the lake. Indeed, one area of the lake known as Indian Kettles was well known for being a very productive fishing grounds in June due to the large shrimp population at that time. The shrimp stay in the sediments during the day and migrate upward every evening to feed on suspended phytoplankton (plants such as algae) or zooplankton (animals which feed on the algae). As the daylight comes, they slowly drop back to the sediments. Many forms of life follow this daily migration: Smaller fish, such as smelt and cisco, follow the shrimp, as do larger fish, right up the food chain.

As the lake trout grow, they begin to feed on other fish. The deepwater sculpin becomes a very important source of food as the trout mature. Sculpin live in deep water, hiding around rocky areas. When other food is scarce lake trout can be found around these areas; in fact, trout may scrape their mouths raw foraging for sculpin. As the lake trout mature they take all types of fish for food, though they prefer soft-rayed fish such as cisco or smelt. (They certainly eat fish such as perch, but the bony fins deter them. In years where large numbers of yellow perch fry are available, the trout will gorge on them while the water is cold enough.) Once the water warms up in June, lake trout descend into the deeper and colder water until mid to late fall, when they begin to congregate prior to the spawning season. They seem to lose most of their appetite at this time and only strike when coaxed by a particularly tantalizing presentation.

In the 1800s and into the early part of this century, lake trout were caught mainly by trolling by rowboat (or later with a motor boat), using linen line weighted with window sash weights. (These weights can still be found around reefs where they were caught up in the rocks.) With the advent of electric motors, the copper wire used as windings became very popular for fishing. The cloth lines stretched, which made it extremely difficult to feel the bottom or a small fish. Wire did not stretch, so the bottom, debris, or small fish could be readily felt. Typically, a 10- to 30-foot leader was used with a light spoon with a hook that faced upward. Fishermen would drop their copper line around one hand, giving the lures an action suggestive of a wounded baitfish.

As gasoline motors became available, rowing (which helped impart a natural action to the trolled lure) gave way to jigging the lure to simulate the same action. Some people, such as Seth Green (the father of America's fish hatcheries), developed specialized wire lines which had swivels every 20 to 30 feet so that multiple leaders and spoons could be fished at one time. One popular rig used old Victoria phonographs and their springs to reel and unreel the wire. To maximize the numbers of lures, some rigs were strung behind the boats with containers as floats, strung with multiple wire lines.

The first homemade lures often were made from the family's silver spoons, undoubtedly causing some major arguments. They were pounded into thin, streamlined shapes by the individual users for the best effect. Thus the name "spoons" came to be used as a type of fishing lure. These lures were highly developed and prized and usually were kept in leather or deerskin bags to protect them from scratches. The first "dodgers" also were developed in this way—a short leader was put on the lure and tied flies were dragged behind the spoon; a natural action was imparted to the fly from the action of the lure.

In the 1940s, lake trout were severely threatened by a new problem—DDT. The eggs of the lake trout, which had been used extensively for a brood stock for other Adirondack lakes, began to die. From 1944 to 1955, abnormal development caused large numbers of the fry to die. The effects of DDT on various organisms were just being discovered, and it was suspected that it was responsible for the fry abnormalities. The DDT was being applied by the DEC and private individuals for the control of the gypsy moth, mosquitoes, and black flies. As the usage increased, so did the problems with the fry.

On March 13, 1956, the senior fish pathologist of the Conservation Department, Howard Dean, went to the hatchery at Fortsville to examine some of the fish fry. The pathologist was told that the fry hatched from the Lake George eggs were dying in large numbers. He found many belly up on the surface and on the bottom, while some swam erratically. Within one month, in spite of all efforts, almost all the 347,900 fry were dead. No one knew why.

217

In the fall of 1956, more eggs were collected from Lake George and once again the fry died. By 1958, less than 1 percent of the fry survived. In 1958, biologists attempted to cross the sperm from the Lake George male trout with the eggs of trout from other lakes and to cross the eggs of Lake George female trout with the sperm from the trout of other lakes in an attempt to locate the reason for the high fry mortality. In every case, when the eggs from the Lake George trout were used, the fry died, indicating the problem was with the female Lake George lake trout.

Several theories were advanced as to the possible cause, such as heredity, radioactivity, or DDT. During my years on the lake, I assisted the Conservation Department's Fisheries Unit in gypsy moth control and fish stocking. Our boats were used to transport pest-control personnel to the islands where gypsy moths existed.

The adverse effects from DDT seemed a probable, but unproved cause of the problem since considerable amounts of DDT dissolved in kerosene had been applied in the Lake George basin. Under contract with the Conservation Department, various airplanes sprayed the entire basin in the 1950s; areas to be sprayed were marked by white cloths placed in trees for aerial identification. At the same time, private groups sprayed other areas of private and public lands. Planes even sprayed directly on the lake. The smell and taste of the DDT and kerosene were distinctive and noted by many anglers.

Both the anglers and the Conservation Department recognized that the lake trout fishing also was declining—many went from getting their daily limits regularly to days without catching a fish.

I had the opportunity to converse with guides regarding the decrease in the numbers of lake trout. Some of these guides were Cecil Lamb, Harry Finkle, Cliff Finkle, Ron Hill, Abner Smith, Charles Peer and Frank Dagles (from the town of Bolton), and Henry Eichin and Joe Briggs (from Lake George Village). Many other guides that I was not personally acquainted with also expressed the same view that the fishing was going downhill. Frank Cotton and Ham Traver, also from Lake George Village, were not professional guides but outstanding fishermen (Ham Traver guided several governors when 48 of them met at the Sagamore Hotel in 1954). The guides all suspected that DDT could be the source of the problems in the 1950s. Following heavy spraying and rainstorms in 1957, private divers found huge quantities of adult lake trout dead on the bottom of Lake George. (Since these fish live in deep water, when they die they sink to the bottom instead of floating to the top.)

The Conservation Department continued to monitor the hatching of the lake trout fry in 1960, 1961, and 1962. Dr. George E. Burdick, supervisor of aquatic biology at the Conservation Department, published a paper in 1962 that proved DDT was indeed the culprit responsible for the fish kills. Concentrations in excess of 350 parts per million were found in the eggs and in the fatty tissue of the lake trout, and the studies revealed that the fish the trout preyed upon for food— cisco and lake whitefish—also had very high concentrations of DDT.

As a part of this study, fish and eggs were collected from various lakes, including Seneca, Raquette, Fourth, Seventh, and Eighth of the Fulton Chain, as well as Big Moose, Blue Mountain, Saranac, Placid, Schroon, Paradox, and Lake George. These lakes all had significant amounts of DDT applied in their watersheds, and they also had native and stocked lake trout. The studies revealed that the fry collected from Lake George, Fourth, and Schroon Lakes all had concentrations of DDT sufficient to result in complete mortality of the fry.

The studies finally determined why the fry died and why the DDT eventually killed even the adult fish, especially the lake trout. DDT is what is now known as a bioaccumulator—a relatively small dosage applied to the land or water is retained in each step of the food chain and accumulates in animals higher in it. While the water may have only had 0.35 parts per billion of DDT, algae gathered up to 1000 times more, the animal plankton gathered more, and the lake trout gathered still more. The final concentration was thus as much as 350 parts per million. (The recommended limit for dietary intake of fish is now less than 5 parts per million—thus humans who ate these fish also accumulated even larger concentrations. The effect on us is unknown.) Additionally, DDT is not water soluble, but it is fat soluble. The fry, which showed the first problems, fed off the yolk sac

219

attached to them at birth for the first month or more—it contains high concentrations of fat. Concentrations of DDT in yolk fat correlated almost perfectly with mortality of the fry from each lot. In 1963, the use of DDT was banned in the Lake George basin and was subsequently banned on all lands supervised by the Conservation Department in 1967.

Unfortunately, the problem did not disappear with the ban. Virtually no natural lake trout reproduction had occurred for almost 10 years. The DDT also was still in the sediments and in the food chain, so more years went by before the DDT slowly broke down and was eliminated through the food chain. Lake trout were stocked from strains that did not have high concentrations of DDT, but the forage fish were not stocked—lake whitefish is now extinct from the Lake George basin, and the cisco also was decimated, though not completely wiped out. During the 1950s, guides Frank Dagles, Charles Peer, Harry Finkle, Kevin Conerty, Cecil Lamb, and I actually observed hundreds of ciscoes belly up on the surface and others swimming very erratically. I remember one sandy beach area where one could actually shovel up the dead ciscoes. Only in the 1990s has the population showed a return to levels of the 1950s. At that time schools of up to 50 acres were seen near the surface in the late spring, with larger fish swimming through them in search of food. We can only hope that the population will continue to grow.

The deaths of these forage fish created another problem: There was too small a forage base to support the remaining lake trout and stocked fish, and their growth rates suffered for many years. For example, fish that would have been six to eight pounds were only three to four pounds.

As a consequence of these findings, New York State issued an outright ban on DDT in 1971; later the federal government prohibited its manufacture and distribution in the United States.

The next significant event associated with trout populations in Lake George involved the introduction of a new forage species, the rainbow smelt. The smelt never were a species associated with Lake George, and the species is suspected to have been purposely

220

introduced around 1970. It has been alleged that certain individuals introduced the smelt for the sole purpose of providing food for the trout and salmon, but the rumor that makes the most sense is that burlap bags were placed in streams of Raquette Lake when smelt were spawning there; when the bags were covered with eggs and milt, they were transported to the Lake George basin and put in some streams. The smelt were officially documented in 1973, but had been present for some years prior. They have since proliferated to all the streams and appear to be spawning in the lake to some degree. They have been very beneficial to the lake trout and salmon populations. The growth rates of the trout and salmon have increased greatly since their introduction. Although they certainly have helped as a food source, they show large changes in their population levels from year to year due to the fact that they primarily reproduce in streams. Lake George does not have large streams and the ones present generally are very steep, thus limiting the distance that fish can climb before depositing their eggs. The streams also have large differences in their annual flow and temperature. Some years the smelt have very good reproduction; in some years the reproduction is poor. The adult population is thus also highly variable. All stream-spawning species in Lake George basin have the same problems. A long-term forage base is dependent on the lake-spawning species that are not dependent upon the varying runoff and rain of out area.

The smelt became a very popular source of bait in Lake George. Fisherman netted them live from the streams in the 1970s and used them in the spring as live bait. They also used them as dead bait in various trolling rigs in the summer and again as dead bait on tip-ups in the winter. The smelt were very effective and were banned in the late 1970s as bait. They were also highly valued as food by many people and were netted, cleaned, and eaten until 1988. At that time, netting was banned since it was decided that the smelt were more valuable as a forage species for the trout and salmon than as a food resource for humans. The lake trout like them so much that reports of two dozen smelt in a lake trout stomach with one sticking out the mouth when caught were not unheard of. Prior to the introduction of the smelt, it was not uncommon to find large lake trout with as many as four to six recently stocked trout or salmon in their stomachs.

By the 1980s, the lake trout had begun reproducing again in sufficient numbers, and it was no longer necessary to stock them. At this time, the minimum "keeper" size was increased from 15 to 18 inches; later, the biologists determined that it would improve the fishing more if the lake trout were allowed to reproduce longer and the size was raised to the present limit of 21 inches.

The next action by the DEC was to lower the overall creel limit of the trout and salmon from three per person per day to two. At the present time, the DEC is considering raising the size limit of the landlocked salmon to 21 inches or to reduce the creel limit for that species.

The lake trout have now returned to Lake George in numbers and size that rival any recorded fishing. In the 1970s, a 19-pound, 3-ounce landlocked salmon was caught; in 1997, a seven-year-old caught a 26-pound, 7-ounce lake trout. Since then, a 32-pound trout also was reported, and each year there are at least a half dozen reported over 20 pounds.

Unfortunately, landlocked salmon are not doing quite as well in the lake. They are dependent on stocking, not natural reproduction, since they cannot reproduce in sufficient numbers to populate the lake. Problems with hatchery-raised fish and high fishing pressure through the year have greatly reduced the number of large salmon caught.

Continued management efforts by the DEC and the various groups concerned with the fish in Lake George should help to maintain and improve our valuable natural resources. It is vital that we maintain the environment appropriately for future generations and manage it for all to enjoy.

FREEZE-OVERS
AND ICE-OUTS

E VERY WINTER, *almost* without exception, Lake George undergoes a wonderful and remarkable transformation as it changes— sometimes slowly and sometimes literally overnight—from water to ice. Suddenly the lake is no longer a huge black mirror on still days and nights, and no longer a rippling sea of sparkling diamonds when the wind churns its waters. Instead, it is transformed into a giant, flat, white field. As the ice grows in thickness, sometimes reaching more than three feet during extremely cold winters, the modes of transportation and the recreational activities on the lake change. The "waters" are dotted with fishermen, iceboats, cross-country skiers, and even cars and trucks.

During this century, records have been kept of the dates when the lake froze over and when it melted. These records of freeze-overs and ice-outs often vary, depending on who is doing the recording, since the lake might freeze over, break up, and then refreeze at a later date. My own criteria for ice-out is a traditional one, dating back to an era when steamboats were the predominate mode of transportation on the lake. Using this standard, ice-out occurs when a boat can navigate from the Lake George Steamboat Dock in Lake George Village through the Narrows and Mother Bunch Islands to Baldwin, the home of the Lake George Steamboat Company's dry dock and the most northern mooring for the company's boats. Conversely, freeze- over occurs when a boat cannot make this same voyage.

Records for ice-outs and freeze-overs were kept by John Stickney of Bolton Landing from 1907 to 1939. The Warren County Department of Public Works continued Stickney's records from 1940 until the present. According to these records, there were only four winters in this century during which the lake did not completely

223

freeze. These were the winters of 1918–1919, 1990–1991, 1994–1995, and 1997–1998. The records also show that the lake froze over in December 3 times, in January 71 times, and in February 13 times. The earliest freeze-over on record was December 20, 1980, while the latest was February 29, 1932.

Ice-outs occurred 6 times in March, 78 times in April, and twice in May. The earliest ice-out took place on March 21, 1983, and the latest on May 2, 1940.

The average freeze-over date is January 14, while the average ice-out date is April 15. This means that the average length of time the lake is frozen is 90 days, or one quarter of the calendar year.

ICE SAFETY

Travel on Lake George just prior to ice-out or just after freeze-over can be very dangerous. The rule of thumb is that four inches of ice is sufficient to hold a man's weight if the air temperature is below freezing and continues that way. One should follow the same guidelines when walking on ice as when navigating a boat: stay clear of shoals, reefs, shoreline points and islands. Always stay well away from bubbler systems and ice eaters—devices used to keep areas around docks and shorelines free of ice—and avoid areas of strong current such as stream outlets and certain channels in the lake.

The color of the ice is a good indicator of its ability to support weight. A general rule of ice safety is that blue ice—water which has frozen just as it does in your ice cube trays at home—is safe. Snow ice, on the other hand, is not safe to venture out on—it is frozen wet snow, also called slush. Black ice, which is newly formed and transparent, does not occur every year. When it does form, it is usually only in certain patches on the lake. Walking on transparent black ice is a unique experience, providing a clear view of the cracks and bubbles as well as the lake's bottom up to a depth of at least 20 feet, and occasionally even a fish frozen in the ice.

Without a doubt, the frozen waters harbor many mysteries which cannot be scientifically explained. In 1991, although the lake was supposedly solidly frozen, there was an area north of West Dollar

Island continuing to Hatchet Island which did not completely freeze over. Many snowmobilers and fishermen, trying to find an explanation for this phenomenon, were stumped.

Individuals who venture out onto the ice during safe freeze-overs often experience rumbles and other eerie sounds which can be unnerving to the uninitiated. These noises, which some have described as being similar to those of a minor earthquake, are caused by the stress and pressure of the expanding ice sheets.

PRESSURE RIDGES

Pressure ridges, also known as pressure cracks or heaves, lift the ice upward. These cracks occur as the freezing water expands and the ice pushes upward, forming a long ridge. The upward heaving of a pressure crack eases the tension in another area, causing the ice to pull apart and resulting in open water.

Pressure ridges are less frequent in years of heavy snowfalls because the snow insulates the ice, protecting it from contraction and expansion. The locations of pressure ridges vary from year to year. In fact, fishermen told me that the incomplete 1995 freeze-over revealed pressure ridges where they never would have expected them. The pressure ridges also have been known to push downward below the surface of the normal ice sheets.

Pressure ridges are a danger to snowmobilers and other vehicles. The raised areas of the ice act as a low fence, preventing passage and restricting the usable area. Iceboats and snowmobiles may catch a runner, or the ice, which is weak at that particular point, may break under the weight of the vehicle.

Caution should always be exercised near a pressure ridge. Wet spots and areas of cracked ice should be avoided at all times. These ridges usually increase in size, both in depth as well as in their length along the ice's surface, since the ice continues to expand as long as it is free of snow. Once there is a snow cover of more than two inches, everyone should stay well away from any pressure ridges, since the ice here thickens at a greatly reduced rate. A snow cover of two to three inches insulates the ice, preventing it from growing any thicker. If the ice was not thick enough for safe passage before a snowstorm, it definitely will not be safe after the snowstorm. Many times over the years I have watched as newly formed ice, insulated by a blanket of snow, was broken up by a heavy wind.

The area south of Montcalm Point is noted for ice breakups after freeze-overs although areas just a mile to the north or south, protected from the heavy winds and the melting action of the surface waves, might have at least five inches of good, solid ice.

WHEN PUSH COMES TO SHOVE

Damage to docks, boathouses, and shorelines can result from what is known as "ice pushes." A sheet of ice which is free of snow thickens rapidly, while at the same time expanding. This expansion pushes the entire weight of the ice toward the shore, producing enormous pressure. As the ice cools during the night, it contracts. This decrease in size stresses the ice cover, causing cracks to develop. Water seeps into the cracks and freezes. When the sun rises, the ice is warmed and expands slowly.

Ice breaking onto Three Brother Islands.   *Photo courtesy Pat and Dick Swire*

During the day, the ice expands, resulting in new fractures. Again, water seeps into the cracks and freezes, enlarging the ice cover even more. As this daily heating and cooling of the ice sheet continues and the ice cover increases in size, the pressure also increases. The severity of damage to docks, boathouses and the shoreline is directly related to the thickness of the ice at the shore.

ICE-OUTS

Throughout the winter, despite snowfalls, rain, or temperature changes, the ice cover continues to thicken as the water below the ice freezes and the water-saturated snow on top of the ice cover turns to ice. This is known as frozen slush or snow ice.

When spring arrives, the snow layers on top of the ice melt first. Thus, the lake's ice cover has water below it as well as water on top of it. The ice mass retains a constant temperature of 32° F. (0° C.) On a cold day, the dry upper surface of the ice may be 10 to 20 degrees colder than the bottom surface, which remains at 32° F. The sun's heat causes a process of internal melting (called candling or honeycombing) whereby the crystals within the ice cover are separated into pieces which resemble long candles. As the warm weather continues, these candles break off and float away in a mass. As the pieces of ice bob in the waves, they produce a tinkling sound reminiscent of thousands of chimes or panes of glass breaking. This lovely sound heralds the coming of spring.

Some people think that the ice cover sinks during the last stages of melting. In fact, many natives of the area have been successful in convincing visitors that this is what actually happens. However, anyone who has ever watched ice cubes melt in a glass of water can tell you that they do not sink. Test it yourself.

If a strong and steady wind blows after the ice breakup, it will push all the ice floes to the shores of the islands and the mainland. These ice floes are generally a combination of honeycombed and solid blue ice as much as four to eight inches thick. These heavy blocks of ice, pushed by the wind, can inflict great damage as they crash against docks, boathouses, and the shoreline.

227

Looking south from 10,000 feet.   © *Richard K. Dean*

228

The Narrows looking north from 10,000 feet.   © *Richard K. Dean*

Many area residents delight in predicting the ice-out date each year, setting up pools and wagering hefty bets. Over the years, the actual date often has been disputed, sometimes leading to considerable friction between the betting parties. It is a good idea, before getting involved in any of these bets, to make sure that the criteria for what actually constitutes ice-out has been clearly defined.

BREAKING THE ICE

I always have had great respect for the dangers of ice conditions on Lake George. Nevertheless, I have had some very close calls on the ice and have learned first-hand just how treacherous and unpredictable this beautiful lake can be.

In the winter of 1972 I drove a state-owned pickup truck out to Glen Island and back, circumventing a long pressure ridge which extended across Northwest Bay almost to Juniper Hills on the main shore. An hour later, I returned to Glen Island, following the same route I had taken earlier. When I was about 200 feet from shore, I suddenly came upon an area of open water with a large slab of ice slanting directly down toward the bottom of the lake. Slamming on my brakes, I went into a skid. In a matter of about 30 seconds I found myself up to my waist in water in the cab of the truck. Fortunately, I was able to climb out of the truck and wade in the water along a slab of ice attached to the slanted slab below. The water was cold but bearable. The alternative was worse.

Two men working on the mainland, Rey Anderson Sr. and Francis Granger, seeing what had happened, raced for a rowboat which was pulled up on the shore. They pushed it across the ice toward me and the open water. By the time they reached me, however, I had already made my way to solid ice.

Anderson and Granger brought me to Bolton, where we enlisted the aid of Fred Smith. He immediately set off across the ice in his Jeep and, with the help of Wally Chmura and Rudy Volkmann, began the rescue operation of the pickup truck. Using an ice auger, they bored a hole in the solid ice cover about 100 yards from where the truck lay submerged in water up to its steering wheel. They attached one end of a chain to the Jeep's rear bumper and the other to a crowbar, which they inserted into the hole in the ice. Chmura then jumped into the rowboat, taking with him one end of the cable from the Jeep's winch. When he reached the truck, we watched in disbelief as he tried to open the cab door.

"Wally, what are you doing?" I yelled. "Hook the cable onto the bumper!"

"I've got to get the registration out of the glove compartment," he yelled back.

"To hell with the registration," I screamed at him. "Nobody's going to check that out in 30 feet of water!"

Chmura finally hooked the cable to the rear bumper, and Smith slowly winched the truck back onto solid ice. I learned a valuable lesson from this experience: Never ever take anything for granted when it comes to ice conditions.

ICE FOR REFRIGERATION

From the mid-nineteenth to the early twentieth century, ice harvesting was an important industry on Lake George, providing jobs for many men who otherwise would have been unemployed during the long winter months.

Before the advent of bottled gas and electric refrigeration at Glen Island, the responsibility of harvesting ice for the headquarters and the store on that island fell to the forest rangers. From the 1920s to the 1950s, Glen Island had an icehouse. One of the jobs of the CCC in 1938 was to construct a new icehouse on that island. The old-timers who maintained the private icehouses for the summer estates and commercial establishments could always be relied upon to help us ascertain the ice's thickness, the location of pressure ridges, and the safest routes for travel on the ice. We were indeed fortunate in being able to take advantage of their experience and knowledge of the lake.

In January 1942, the day before our planned ice harvest, Conservation Department employees Claude Carey, Ken Morehouse, and I headed out across the ice toward Glen Island in a three-quarter-ton pickup truck. When we were about half way across Northwest

231

Bay, we noticed a huge pressure ridge ahead of us. The ridge was about four feet high and extended all the way to the shoreline of Northwest Bay. With two feet of open water surrounding it, there was no way we could get around this pressure ridge.

Carey came up with the idea of building a bridge across the gap. We drove back to shore, returning with wooden planks, ice chisels, and saws. The planks were laid across the open water and then packed with slush in the hope that it would freeze up overnight. We also sawed and chiseled the pressure ridge at that point to make it level with the ice sheet. When we returned the next morning, we found that Mother Nature had cooperated. The improvised bridge was firmly entrenched, and two trucks carrying department employees drove across it, delivering the workers safely to Glen Island for the ice harvest.

We generally harvested 150 blocks of ice, enough to supply the two residents of the Glen Island headquarters as well as the commissary for five months. The ice should be at least 12 inches thick before it can be harvested. Generally, however, the blocks we cut were 20 inches thick. It generally took two days to harvest and insulate the ice with sawdust.

CURRENT EVENTS

I had another close call on the ice during the harvest of 1946. After filling the Glen Island ice house, Claude Carey, Ken Morehouse, and I were assigned the task of returning the motorized ice saw which we borrowed each year from Ernest Granger, the caretaker of the Knapp property on the east side of the lake. Our destination was the Knapps' icehouse, just south of Elsa Steinback's home on Shelving Rock. Towing the ice saw behind our pickup truck, we headed toward the channel between Fourteen Mile Island and the mainland. Before entering the channel, however, we thought it might be a good idea to test the thickness of the ice. A test hole drilled with our ice auger revealed that the ice was only two to three inches thick at that point—not enough to hold a man's weight, much less that of a pickup truck.

Since we had just been harvesting the ice, we knew that in the middle of the lake it was about 20 inches thick. We were very surprised to find it suddenly so thin here. I later learned, however, that the thin ice in that channel is caused by a current which flows between the mainland and Fourteen Mile Island. We made a detour and arrived safely at our destination via a different route, one with good, solid ice. The realization of how close we came to losing our truck (and perhaps our lives) still sends shivers down my spine. In February 1996, a snowmobiler was unsuccessful in his attempt to go through this channel. He narrowly escaped drowning.

The channel at Fourteen Mile Island is not the only area of the lake where currents are prevalent. They also are found in the channel under the bridge to Green Island, between the Tongue Mountain shoreline and Turtle Island, between Clay Island and Homer Point, and around the Waltonian group of islands in Hague.

Although through the years there have been some catastrophes and even more near-catastrophes on the ice of Lake George, and many summer residents have returned to find their docks and boathouses ravaged by it, the ice also brings joy to the thousands of residents and visitors who enjoy winter sports such as ice fishing, skating, ski-sailing, iceboating, cross-country skiing, and last, but not least, the activities of the annual Lake George Winter Festival held each February in Lake George Village, weather permitting.

The ice conditions of early 1996 were unique—the lake froze over completely in just one night on January 4. This type of quick freeze is practically unheard of and resulted in unusual pressure ridges and cracks. In addition, there was not enough snow to blanket the ice and insulate it from the sun. About two weeks later, we experienced a thaw accompanied by unusually heavy rains. This caused the hundreds of holes bored by the ice fishermen to expand, creating a dangerous situation. Fortunately, there were no mishaps.

I close out this chapter on the lake's ice characteristics with the following wish: May Mother Nature be kind and gentle and may the wind be always at your back during ice-out.

Freezing and Thawing Records

WINTER SEASON	FREEZE-OVER	ICE-OUT
1907–08	January 31	April 6
1908–09	January 14	April 14
1909–10	January 8	April 12
1910–11	January 10	April 11
1911–12	January 22	April 12
1912–13	January 16	March 27
1913–14	January 14	April 22
1914–15	January 1	April 12
1915–16	February 16	April 19
1916–17	January 12	April 19
1917–18	January 1	April 14
1918–19	Did not freeze	
1919–20	January 6	April 20
1920–21	February 12	April 8
1921–22	January 3	April 12
1922–23	January 7	April 22
1923–24	January 28	April 14
1924–25	January 9	April 3
1925–26	January 16	April 24
1926–27	January 3	April 8
1927–28	January 30	April 8
1928–29	January 27	April 3
1929–30	January 19	April 8
1930–31	January 16	April 10
1931–32	February 29	April 19

WINTER SEASON	FREEZE-OVER	ICE-OUT
1932–33	February 14	April 14
1933–34	January 19	April 19
1934–35	January 5	April 19
1935–36	January 29	April 6
1936–37	February 4	April 16
1937–38	January 13	April 2
1938–39	January 23	April 25
1939–40	January 23	May 2
1940–41	January 10	April 15
1941–42	January 31	April 5
1942–43	January 5	April 23
1943–44	January 2	April 24
1944–45	January 6	March 28
1945–46	January 20	March 28
1946–47	January 13	April 12
1947–48	January 11–12	April 2–3
1948–49	February 3–28	March 29
1949–50	February 6–8	April 18–20
1950–51	January 20–31	April 10–11
1951–52	January 22–28	April 10–12
1952–53	February 5–17	April 3
1953–54	January 14–18	April 10–12
1954–55	January 22–29	April 11–12
1955–56	January 14–25	April 12
1956–57	January 14	April 9
1957–58	January 18–21	April 11
1958–59	January 8–9	April 18–19
1959–60	Jan. 12–Feb. 5	April 17
1960–61	January 5–19	April 9–22
1961–62	January 20–22	April 13
1962–63	January 4–19	April 16–17
1963–64	January 7	April 15
1964–65	January 15	April 20–21

WINTER SEASON	FREEZE-OVER	ICE-OUT
1965–66	Jan. 12–Feb. 27	April 11–15
1966–67	February 7–8	April 10–11
1967–68	January 9	April 2–3
1968–69	January 13	April 11–12
1969–70	January 8	April 19
1970–71	January 9	May 1–2
1971–72	January 22	April 29
1972–73	January 9	April 1–2
1973–74	January 18	April 16–17
1974–75	February 4	April 19
1975–76	January 13	April 7–8
1976–77	December 28	April 6–9
1977–78	January 19	April 22
1978–79	January 11	March 31
1979–80	January 31	April 11
1980–81	December 20	April 7
1981–82	January 13	April 20
1982–83	February 10	March 21
1983–84	December 24	April 13
1984–85	January 17	April 6
1985–86	January 25	April 7
1986–87	January 27	April 6
1987–88	February 7	April 7
1988–89	February 3	April 15
1989–90	December 23	April 12
1990–91	Did not freeze	
1991–92	January 14	April 20
1992–93	January 25	April 17
1993–94	January 10	April 23
1994–95	Did not freeze	
1995–96	January 5	April 8
1996–97	January 14	April 18
1997–98	Did not freeze	

ABOUT THE AUTHOR

Frank Leonbruno was born in Whitehall, birthplace of the United States Navy which fought the British on Lake George during the Revolutionary War. He began his career on Lake George in 1935 when he joined the Civilian Conservation Corps. In 1941 he started working for the New York State Conservation Department, later renamed the Department of Environmental Conservation. He retired from the DEC in 1983, having been supervisor of Lake George operations since 1973. He has served his community and the Town of Bolton well—as president of the Bolton Central School Board; as town councilman, and town and county supervisor; and as a member of the Bolton Volunteer Fire Company. Has also has been a past director of the Lake George Association. *Lake George Reflections* continues Frank Leonbruno's dedication and devotion to his beloved Lake George.

ABOUT THE EDITOR

Ginger Henry was born in Ticonderoga and spent much of her childhood in Hague. She has worked as a political speech writer in Washington, and as a journalist, editor and translator both in the U. S. and in Germany, where she lived for over twenty years before moving back to Hague in 1995. She now lives and works in the Boston area, returning to her log cabin on the shores of Lake George as frequently as possible. Her family's island connections date back to the nineteenth century, when her great grandfather, James Buchanan Henry, purchased Green Island in Bolton. Ginger's mother, Dottie Henry, is the publisher of Hague's monthly newspaper, *The Hague Chronicle*.